Through the Eye of the Needle

Counsel for Spiritual
Survival in the Last Days

By

Shaykh Nazim Adil Al-Haqqani

Foreword By
Shaykh Muhammad Hisham Kabbani

INSTITUTE FOR SPIRITUAL AND CULTURAL ADVANCEMENT

Library of Congress Cataloging-in-Publication Data

Published and Distributed by:
Institute for Spiritual and Cultural Advancement

17195 Silver Parkway, #401
Fenton, MI 48430 USA
Tel: (888) 278-6624
Fax:(810) 815-0518
Email: staff@naqshbandi.org
Web:
http://www.naqshbandi.org

First Edition December 2007
ISBN: 1-930409-34-6

Shaykh Nazim Adil al-Haqqani (right) with his disciple of fifty years, Shaykh Muhammad Hisham Kabbani. Head of the world's largest Naqshbandi Sufi spiritual order, Shaykh Nazim is known for his life-altering lessons in how to discipline the ego, reach a state of spiritual surrender, and achieve true liberation from the bondage of worldly distraction and pursuit. Shaykh Hisham Kabbani, Shaykh Nazim's deputy, accompanies the venerable shaykh on his many visits to various regions of the world, where they meet with political and religious leaders, media, and throngs of common folk.

TABLE OF CONTENTS

FOREWORD

Bismillahi-r-Rahmani-r-Rahim
In the Name of God, the Most Beneficent, the Most Merciful

All praise is due to God Almighty, Allah the Exalted and Bounteous and the most fluent, abundant and sweet praise and blessings be upon His perfect servant, the mercy to all creation and exemplar of perfect character, ethics and morality Prophet Muhammad ,[1] and upon his family and Companions.

This book is a compendium of *sohbets* or spiritual discourses by our master—chief of saints and reviver of the Prophetic path to divine enlightenment, teacher of millions and worldwide leader of the Naqshbandi-Haqqani Sufi Order, Mawlana Shaykh Muhammad Nazim Adil al-Haqqani, may Allah grant him health and long life.

It is related that in the Last Days of this world—which, based upon the predicted indications is taking place even as I pen these words—those who adhere to the pure teachings of the prophets and saints will become rare. On the contrary, those who breach the Prophetic Tradition, the Sunnah, will be commonplace.

No prior prophet ever mentioned in such detail what Prophet Muhammad foretold fourteen hundred years

---

[1] stands for *"Salla-Lahu 'alayhi wa sallam,"* meaning, "Allah's peace and blessings be upon him," the Islamic invocation for Prophet Muhammad .

ago. In the seventh century, he gave a precise description with specific details which were not fully understood until their manifestation in the present age. The Prophet ﷺ explained what would transpire in the Last Days so that the people witnessing those events could recognize their place in time. The Prophet ﷺ warned that when bedouin Arabs compete to construct lofty buildings in the desert the Hour of Judgment would be close. He predicted that in the Last Days, trustworthy people would be vilified regarded as traitors by the people.

In a Prophet Tradition[2] it is related that a bedouin came to Prophet Muhammad ﷺ and asked when Judgment Day would take place. He said, "When the trust (al-amana) is lost, then await Judgment Day." The bedouin asked, "How will it be lost?" The Prophet ﷺ replied, "When power and authority comes in the hands of unfit persons, then wait for the Judgment Day."[3] He also has said that "the trustworthy one will be called a traitor."

As the Prophet ﷺ predicted, the psychology of people in our time is the opposite of what is prescribed and it is nearly impossible to find a trustworthy person. At the same time, everywhere on earth, different groups are busy destroying what remains of faith and spirituality, each one following its own agenda. Even "spiritual" groups and individuals slander each other, and through their corrupt behavior, support falsehood — all the while claiming to be believers.

The words of the tradition, "The trustworthy, al-amin, one will be said to be a traitor," has an interpretation. Al-

---

[2] Arabic: *hadith.*

[3] *Sahih Bukhari.*

Amin is one of the names of Prophet Muhammad ﷺ, and one of the signs of the Last Days is that people will attack the Prophets of God, in particular the Last Messenger, Muhammad ﷺ, and the message he brought for mankind's felicity.

Alhamdulillah—praise God—we are fortunate to be students or disciples of Mawlana Shaykh Nazim. As long as he, and Sufi masters like him, continue to teach the ways of the the prophets and saints, hope remains for humankind. For his teachings, while outwardly plain, are endowed with a wisdom and grace seldom found today. The shaykh's words take you back to a simpler time, when people were straightforward, when they what they meant, and when they did what they said.

May God bless you as you pick up this volume and read some of the holy teachings he has brought. It is well known in the Naqshbandi Sufi tradition, that pure words of guidance are able to elevate the reader to the stations and states described simply through the blessed character, *baraka*, of one authorized to teach them. Futher, these teachings will remain with you and part of you in this life and on, into the hereafter.

I am only a student and I have been learning from my teacher Mawlana Shaykh Nazim, who, despite his 85 years of age is still incredibly active spreading the teachings that come to his heart from the spiritual "central headquarters." What I saw and learned from my master I cannot express because those fountains are always pouring forth, continuously flowing. The hearts of such saints are like waterfalls: giving always and they are not asking to take anything, asking only to give.

As the world around us seems to slide further into its darkest chapter, in a time when negativity and skepticism insistently challenge faith, the faithful of all beliefs seek a beacon that will lead them to a divine shelter of peace and protection. Presented in this volume are essential aspects of a spiritual discipline which dates back to the time when Prophet Muhammad delivered the divine message—a message preserved by Sufi masters over forty generations.

In these times when Islam is more and more visible on the world stage, it is hoped through this humble work that readers will come to better understand the true teachings of Islam, namely, the universal endorsement to practice moderation and follow the middle course, to hold patience, to uphold tolerance and respect for others, to approach conflict resolution in peaceful ways, to condemn all forms of terrorism, and above all, to love God, appreciate His Divine favors, and strive in His divine service. The greatest Islamic teaching is that there is no higher station than to serve the Lord Almighty.

Shaykh Muhammad Hisham Kabbani
Fenton, Michigan
October 28, 2007

INTRODUCTION

Endless praise and thanks be to God Most High, who guides His servants to His light by means of other servants of His whose hearts He illuminates with His divine love.

Since the beginning of human history, God Most High has conveyed His revealed guidance to mankind through His prophets and messengers, beginning with the first man, Adam ﷺ. The prophetic line includes such well-known names as Noah, Abraham, Ishmael, Isaac, Jacob, Joseph, Lot, Moses, David, Solomon, and Jesus, peace be upon them all, ending and culminating in Muhammad, the Seal of the Prophets ﷺ, a descendant of Abraham ﷺ, ﷺwho brought the final revelation from God to all mankind.

But although there are no longer prophets upon the earth, the Most Merciful Lord has not left His servants without inspired teachers and guides. *Awliya*—holy people or saints—are the inheritors of the prophets. Up to the Last Day, these "friends of God," the radiant beacons of truth, righteousness and the highest spirituality, will continue in the footsteps of the prophets, calling people to their Lord and guiding seekers to His glorious Divine Presence.

One such inspired teacher, a shaykh or *murshid* of the Naqshbandi Sufi Order, is Shaykh Nazim Adil al-Qubrusi al-Haqqani. A descendant not only of the Holy Prophet Muhammad ﷺ but also of the great Sufi masters 'Abul Qadir Gilani and Jalaluddin Rumi, Shaykh Nazim was born in Larnaca, Cyprus, in 1922 during the period of British rule of the island. Gifted from earliest childhood with an extraordinarily spiritual personality, Shaykh Nazim received his spiritual training in Damascus at the hands of Maulana Shaykh 'Abdullah ad-Daghestani (fondly referred to as "Grandshaykh"), the mentor of such well-known figures as Gurjieff and J. G. Bennett, over a period of forty years.

Before leaving this life in 1973, Grandshaykh designated Shaykh Nazim as his successor. In 1974, Shaykh Nazim went to London for the first time, thus initiating what was to become a yearly practice during the month of Ramadan up to 1990s. A small circle of followers began to grow around him, eagerly taking their training in the ways of Islam and *tariqah* at his hands.

From this humble beginning, the circle has grown to include thousands of *murids* or disciples in various countries of the world, among whom are to be found many eminent individuals, both religious and secular. Shaykh Nazim is a luminous, tremendously impressive spiritual personality, radiating love, compassion and goodness. He is regarded by many of his *murids* as the *qutub* or chief saint of this time.

The shaykh teaches through a subtle interweaving of personal example and talks ("Associations" or *sohbets*), invariably delivered extempore according to the inspirations that are given to him. He does not lecture, but rather pours out from his heart into the hearts of his listeners such knowledge and wisdoms as may change their innermost beings and bring them toward their Lord as His humble, willing, loving servants.

Shaykh Nazim's language and style are unique, so eloquent, moving and flavorful that not only do his teachings seem inspired but also his extraordinary use of words. His *sohbets* represent the teachings of a twentieth century Sufi master, firmly grounded in Islamic orthodoxy, speaking to the hearts of the seekers of God of any faith tradition from his own great, wide heart, in a tremendous outpouring of truth, wisdom and divine knowledge which is surely unparalleled in the English language, guiding the seeker toward the Divine Presence.

The sum total of Shaykh Nazim's message is that of hope, love, mercy and reassurance. In a troubled and uncertain world in which old, time-honored values have given place to new ones of confused origins and unclear prospects, in which a feeling heart and thinking mind is constantly troubled by a sense of things being terribly disordered and out of control, in which the future seems forebodingly dark and uncertain for humanity, he proclaims God's love and care for His servants, and invites them to give their hearts to Him.

Shaykh Nazim holds out to seekers the assurance that even their smallest steps toward their Lord will not go unnoticed and unresponded to. Rather than threatening sinners with the prospect of eternal Hell, he offers hope of salvation from the Most Merciful Lord, and heart-warming encouragement and incentive for inner change and growth. As one who has traversed every step of the seeker's path and reached its pinnacle, he offers both inner and practical guidelines for attaining the highest spiritual goals.

Volumes One through Five in this series constist of Shaykh Nazim's talks from the Ramadans of 1984 through 1988, while Volume Six consists of a number of talks given on other occasions in various years. Each of these talks is entirely extempore, as Shaykh Nazim never prepares his words but invariably speaks according to inspirations coming to his heart.

In keeping with the shaykh's methodology—the methodology of the prophets, particularly of the Last Prophet, Muhammad, peace be upon him and upon them all, and of the Qur'an itself—of reinforcing vital lessons by repetition and reiteration, the same themes and anecdotes recur again and again. The talks seem to come in unannounced clusters, centering around a primary theme, which develops and evolves according to the spiritual state of the listeners. Thus, Shaykh Nazim may cite the same verse or *hadith*, or tell the same tale on different occasions, each time reinforcing a slightly different aspect of the eternal message of love and light which is Islam.

The shaykh's talks are interspersed with words and phrases from Arabic and other Islamic languages. These are translated either in the text itself, in footnotes the first time they occur, or, for general and recurrent terms, in the Glossary at the end of this volume. Qur'anic verses quoted in the text have been referenced for easy access.

Every attempt has been made to retain the shaykh's original language with minimal editing. However, since these talks were transcribed from audio tapes recorded on amateur equipment by listeners for their own personal use (or, in the case this volume, by a *murid* extremely familiar with the shaykh's language and ideas, by hand), some inadvertent errors may have found their way into the text. For these, we ask Allah's forgiveness and your kind indulgence. May He fill your heart with light and love as you read and reflect upon these inspired words, and guide you safely to His exalted Divine Presence.

PUBLISHER'S NOTE

Shaykh Nazim is fluent in Arabic, Turkish and Greek, and semi-fluent in Engish. Over three decades, his llectures have been transated into twenty or more languages, and to date have reached the furthest corners of the globe. We sincerely hope the reader will appreciate the author's unique language style, which has been painstakingly preserved in this work.

As some of the terms in this book may be foreign, to assist the reader we have provded transliterations, as well as a detailed glossary.

NOTES

The following symbols are universally recognized and have been respectfully included in this work:

The symbol ﷺ represents *sall-Allahu 'alayhi wa sallam* (Allah's blessings and greetings of peace be upon him), which is customarily recited after reading or pronouncing the holy name of Prophet Muhammad ﷺ.

The symbol ﷺ represents *'alayhi 's-salam* (peace be upon him/her), which is customarily recited after reading or pronouncing the holy names of the other prophets, family members of Prophet Muhammad ﷺ, the pure and virtuous women in Islam, and the angels.

The symbol ؏/؏ represents *radi-Allahu 'anhu/'anha* (may Allah be pleased with him/her), which is customarily recited after reading or pronouncing the holy names of Companions of the Prophet ﷺ.

In the Name of Allah, The Beneficent and The Munificent

This, my English, is strange English. Not everyone can understand because, *subhanallah*, meanings are coming to my heart, and when running in my heart to give to you, I am using any means – from here, from there - bringing any word which may be useful.

I am like a person waiting for water to run out from the faucet. Then, when suddenly it comes, and he knows the water is going to be turned off, stop running, he may take any container – with a no-good shape, broken on one side, or anything he may find there – quickly bringing them to take that water and store it. Therefore, when meanings are coming to my heart, I am trying to explain with any word, which you may understand or not. But you must understand, because we have a saying, "Listeners must be more wise than speakers." Therefore, when inspiration comes, we must explain.

They are living words, not plastic – bananas, plastic; apples, plastic, and grapes. Even if the shapes are not much, they are living, real. When you are going to arrange them in measures, good system; when you are going to be engaged by outside forms, you are losing meanings. ▲

1

BELIEFS BRING PEOPLE TO REALITY

By the name of Allah, All-Mighty, All-Merciful, Most Beneficent and Most Munificent.

A'udhu bil-Lahi min ash-Shaytani-r-rajim. Bismillahi-r-Rahmani-r-Rahim. La haula wa la quwatta illa bil-Lahi-l-'Aliyyi-l-'Adhim.[1] By the name of Allah, Almighty, All-Merciful, Most Beneficent, and Most Munificent.

Subhanak, ya Allah.[2] We are happy, must be happy, with the name of Allah, Almighty, All-Merciful, Most Beneficent and Most Munificent. Exalted, *T'ala,* exalted. *Mutaqaddis,* they can't give any meaning for *taqaddus. Tabarak,* that is coming through the Holy Qur'an for highest respect for Allah Almighty.[3] The words are only suited to the Arabic language. You can't find a similar meaning for one word by another [a synonym] in other languages.[4]

It is an obligation for *mu'mins,* believers, and generally for all mankind, first to learn how they may give their high-

---

[1] "I take refuge with Allah from Satan, the rejected. In the name of Allah, the Beneficent, the Merciful. There is no might nor power except with Allah, the Most High, the Almighty."

[2] "May You be glorified, O Allah."

[3] *Mutaqaddis:* holy, sacred, hallowed, sanctified. *Taqaddus:* hallowing, consecration, sanctification. *Tabarak:* blessed.

[4] That is, it is the nature of Arabic that it conveys multiple meanings or subtle shades of meaning in a single word, such as not found in any other language.

est respect and highest glory to Allah Almighty. That must be for all of mankind who believe in the Lord of the Heavens.

Believing in something, beliefs, is bringing people to an understanding. Of what? You must try to understand. Beliefs bring people to Reality, bringing people to say and to proclaim their belief that *that* is Reality. And what is Reality, that we now know or are trying to know about?

The reality of the existence of the Lord of the Heavens, the existence of Allah, that is Reality, nothing else. Everything else is imagination because real existence is only for Allah. Understand? *That* is reality. It is not what you are imagining and about which you are saying, "That is real"; no. Everything beyond the existence of Allah is nothing, nothing! Beyond Reality, what can you find? Nothing. And real existence is for Allah Almighty only, and that reality must be known.

To say, "I believe in the existence of the Lord and the Creator of all things that we are in"—how are you saying this, O foolish one? Foolish one, to say, "I believe in and I accept the existence of the Lord of the Heavens and the Creator." Who are *you* to say this?" giving to yourself value, importance, by saying, "I believe in God"!

Shahid Allah.[5] Allah, He is the One who Himself is witnessing [to Himself] and giving His proclamation about His existence. "*Shahid Allahu annahu wa malaikatu wa ulu-l-'ilmi,*

---

[5] *"Allah [Himself] bears witness"* (3:18). See footnote 6 for the completion of this verse.

qaiman bil-qist."[6] Allah is witnessing to His own existence, to His own Reality, and it is enough, what He is proclaiming, witnessing to Himself by Himself, for Himself. Unknown, unknown Reality! And you must follow Him and say, "O my God!"

Who are you, who are you, to say, "I believe that there is Allah"? Who are you to say this? You think that you are someone, something, in the Divine Presence, to say, "I believe that there is a God." Oh-oh! If no God, how would you say this, O crazy one?[7] *La haula wa la quwwata illa bil-Lahi-l-'Aliyyi-l-'Adhim*Oh! — "I believe in God"?

This is the level at which some are speaking now; it is a new fashion. Who are you to say this? Say, "O my God!" Say, "*Ya Allah, ya Rabb!*"[8] Say it! If you do not believe in His existence, is He going to go away? No existence for God, Almighty Allah, going away? So many foolish ones, now new fashion, square-headed, empty-headed people, are saying, "We do not believe." Are they not fearing that Allah's anger, L'anat-Ullah, Allah's curse may come on them?

First of all, you must learn, you must understand, you must proclaim, and you must give your highest respect. "Endless glory for my Lord, for my God, who is making me to be in existence, creating me and making me to proclaim His existence, the Exalted."

---

[6]*"Allah [Himself] bears witness that there is no deity except Him, and the angels and people of knowledge, maintaining His creation in justice.* (3:18)

[7]That is, your believing or not believing in God does not affect His existence. Moreover, if there were no God, there would be no "you" to say this..

[8]"O Allah! O Lord!"

Where are people going now—where? Where are you going? Running after Shaytan! Where did Shaytan just bring you, O nations? O mankind living in the twenty-first century, to where have you reached? Do you think that the twenty-first century is the most honored century for you, for mankind? The twenty-first century is making mankind like rubbish, rubbish that is thrown in the dustbin or like rubbish that you put into the toilet.

Shaytan has just brought mankind to that position now, because Shaytan is saying, "Don't say, don't accept Reality." If no Reality, how can anything be? This creation that we are seeing, how can it be in existence? If no one is bringing them into being, how are they going to be in existence? Those empty-headed people may say, "By itself, by themselves. Their existence is through themselves." That is Reality for them, those empty-headed people.

If it is from themselves, how is it that this day is never going to be similar to yesterday, or how is tomorrow going to be different from today? If it is real, "real" never changes. Reality never accepts a change, but others are going to be changed, and sometimes they can be seen but after a while you can't see them. Millions of people may live today, going between East and West, but tomorrow they will not be in the streets or in their homes. No, no more. Millions of people who today are going, coming, doing, acting, tomorrow they will not be in existence. That means their existence is not a real existence. If it were a real existence, they would never disappear; always appearing, must be present.

That means that everything is like a shadow or like a figure in a mirror.[9] The mirror is sending [an image], but what you can see in it is not fixed, always changing. Or a TV screen; each day's events on the screen of a TV are not the same. Where did they go? They went, they finished. If they were real beings, they must be there, never disappearing. But people are not understanding that the existence of a Real One is never going to disappear, never going to finish, to vanish, and must always be in existence.

None of the people that throughout the thousands of years that mankind has lived on this planet, billions of people—now nothing of them. You can find only some *satır*, lines written in books, for some people, and others, never known in their times or afterwards, they are finished. And among those whose names are written in books, there remains only their names and nothing else. That means they were images. Yes? Images. That belongs to imagination, now finished.

You must, when you are looking and seeing these worlds and space and skies and stars and galaxies and so on, millions, billions of those things, you must know something: that all this is running, running, no one knowing

---

[9]The meaning is that only One, the Creator of all things, has true reality, real being, real existence. Whatever He has created is temporal, a material manifestation of His divine will and divine attributes, coming into existence and then disappearing out of materiality by His divine command. Although our souls have an existence beyond the present life, nevertheless, as the products of His divine will and command, we cannot be said to have real existence or real being.

from where it is coming, to where going, coming and disappearing, then finishing.

They are saying now that there are black holes. Millions or billions of stars, when coming near those black holes, the black holes —*pff!* —are swallowing them and no more galaxies are there, finished. If they were real ones, how would black holes swallow and take them and never leave any existence for them, finishing? Where have they gone? If they have real being, how did they disappear? And who put those black holes there?

[Parodies:] "You, Americans, take away this black hole from our way! We must pass through."

"Oh, I can't do that. I may ask the Russians. Perhaps they are putting those black holes. Yeh, look. Ask the Russians."

"We never have time to look at putting black holes. We are looking for white holes, for something to come to us. Ask the Japanese people."

"No, we are a little bit late. You may ask the German people. Their technology is more important."

Then English technologists are saying, "What were we doing for one hundred years? We are searching for Reality, and you are asking about something that disappears. It is not a real thing. You must have something wrong with your eyes. You are looking for a black hole, white hole. Go away!"

Therefore, everything that they are running after, after a while it is disappearing, and when disappearing, finished. They are saying that is like a mirage. From far away, you think there is water and run to it, running, running and coming, looking—"Oh, nothing here," because it was not real. Real is never going to be changed, to be moved; no—fixed! No other power or reality is able to make it move; no. Therefore, real existence is for Allah Almighty and He can do everything. Others, all of them are like figures just appearing on TV screens.

May Allah forgive me, because the twenty-first century's people, they are on the wrong way, wrong way, running after mirages or running to catch imaginary figures, and they can't do that. They must ask about the Real Existence that is never going to be changed or to be taken away. They must learn about the Real Being, the Real Being who is saying, *"Samawat wal-aradin,* all the heavens and earth and everything belongs to Me. I am the Founder. I am the Owner. I am the Creator. I am the Lord. You must seek *that* One."

But the twenty-first century's people are saying, "We are not putting the name of God in our lessons, in our teachings. No room to put His name."

Yes, I know. No room except for Shaytan. You are putting everywhere the name of Shaytan, Shaytan saying, "Don't put any other name. *I* am calling you."

That is the wrong way. They must try to learn about the existence of the Lord of all creation, and He is the only One who can save people here and hereafter. For the honor of the most honored one in His Divine Presence, Sayyidina Muhammad 🕌—*Fateha*. [10] ▲

---

[10]And the good outcome is with Allah. For the honor of [*Surat al-*] *Fatehah*.

2

PUTTING THE OCEAN IN A THIMBLE

A'udhu bil-Lahi min ash-Shaytani-r-rajim. Bismillahi-r-Rahmani-r-Rahim. La haula wa la quwwata illa bil-Lahi-l-'Aliyyi-l-'Adhim.

Only You, O our Lord, can grant us to know, through Your most beloved servant, the most honored servant in Your Divine Presence, who represents Your glory.

Who is that one? Sayyidina Muhammad ﷺ represents the glory of the Lord of the Heavens. No one else; from him all chosen ones are taking glory, chosen ones who are in relationship with the Heavens. If a person does not reach a relationship with the Heavens, no glory and no honor. *Subhanallah*, glory be to Allah! And Sayyidina Muhammad is that one who is granting [glory] on behalf of the Lord of the Heavens, on behalf of all creation and creatures, representing His glory.

Glory is a divine attribute, and if it is not dressed on a person, you can't see it. To be seen, it must be dressed on someone so that people may see, so that his glory may be seen. The glory of the Lord of the Heavens is dressed on Sayyidina Muhammad ﷺ. Whoever does not reach him will never take any glory, here or hereafter. And everyone who is asking for eternal glory must be in relationship with that glorious one. His glory may be seen only on him; otherwise, it is closed, no one knowing. No one could see that glory if that one were not dressed in divine glory, and divine glory, when dressed on him, he becomes glorious. And everyone who reaches to him may be dressed in glory, according to his capacities or abilities.

There are some atoms that scientists are asking to look at through trials, and they are sending a powerful light on them. Then they are coming to be seen on the screen; if taking away that light, they can't be seen. When sending those powerful lights, they can look and see their movements. They can't see their real beings but they may catch their movements and trails; they can understand that there are some beings on that screen. If you are not sending that strong, powerful light on them, they are in darkness; you can't know about their existence. And everyone in creation, also, if divine lights are not sent on them, they can't be seen in existence.

And those who are coming into existence, to take a share of the glory of that glorious one, they must be in relationship with him. Then that glory can be seen on them; otherwise they should be in darkness, no glory. And everyone now who is asking for that glory must search for the way to make a relationship with him. If you do not ask, you are not going to belong to the Prophet ﷺ. If they do not ask to reach and to be in relationship with that glory through that glorious one, they are never going to take glory from the Lord's unlimited Glory Oceans.

The dominions of the Lord of the Heavens are shining with that glory. Dominions are something other than creation, shining. And in all holy books they are mentioned, but if a person does not reach lights, he can't see, can't understand and can't reach to that glory.

Millions of people, they are reciting the Old Testament, from the beginning up to today, as well as millions of people who are reading and looking into the New Testament, but they are never reaching that glory. If one of them had reached that real reaching to Glory Oceans, he couldn't be under the command of anyone except that glorious one. No one can be above those people who have reached glory from the Lord of the Heavens through that most glorious one, the representative of the Lord's Glory Oceans, and he is glorious. They can't reach any lights from Light Oceans, and the greatness and majestic glory can't be dressed on them.

Glory and majesty, that belongs to the dominion of Allah Almighty. This word is a very luminous word in English, "dominion." *Allahu akbar!* Even English-speaking people can't know the real meaning of "dominions". That is an honor that reaches from the Lord of creation to creatures— to belong to the dominions of the Lord of the Heavens. They are reading [about it in the Old and New Testaments]; it is mentioned. And the Last Message in the Holy Qur'an is like oceans; in it you can find out about the dominions of the Lord of the Heavens. But now, if someone reads or looks at the Holy Qur'an, they reading the Holy Qur'an, also, as they would read a newspaper.

Now everyone is carrying a book in their hands and they are saying "Around these pages, there is the meaning of the Holy Qur'an."[11] What is that foolishness? How are you claiming to put Oceans into a coffee cup? *Allahu akbar!* Or tailors are using a thimble, very small. Do you think that Oceans can enter into that thimble? Yet they are claiming that we are putting the Holy Qur'an's meanings around those pages, putting twenty lines around them.

Therefore, everyone is coming, bringing to me [such a Qur'an, and saying,] "O shaykh, we are looking here and we never see what you are saying about that. [Laughter.] From where [did you get it]? This is the verse; this is the meaning. From where are you speaking?"

It is written, it is in it. It is in it, but it is so difficult to reach, to know, to understand, to ask, to love, and to be dressed in that Glory Ocean.

Therefore, people they are ignorant, with their learned ones, called "Doctor". Who is that one? Whether an Anglican Church bishop, doctor, preacher or anyone else, I am saying, "Which holy book mentions the title of 'Doctor'?" Do they find it in the Old Testament or New Testament?

And in their footsteps, our modernized Muslim learned people, they are using that title.[12] "Doctor Ahmad," "Doctor Ahmak," [laughter], and "Doctor Crazy". I am calling to one of them, "Come! What are you doing here?"

---

[11]Referring to the commentaries at the sides or bottom of many editions of the Qur'an.

[12]That is, instead of studying according to established traditional Islamic methods, Muslims are studying Islam and other subjects in order to obtain advanced degrees for worldly purposes in institutions based on secular Western models, from teachers with Western titles and often Western training.

"I have come to give a speech to Muslims."

I am saying, "First, do you know how to clean this mosque? Take this brush and clean it ."

"Shaykh, what you are saying? I am a doctor. I am not servant, to clean a mosque!"

"What is your title?"

"I am a doctor."

"Take my pulse."

"I am not such a doctor."

"Then look at my mind." [Laughter.]

"I don't know how."

"Look my heart."

"No."

From where are Muslims bringing the title of "Doctor"? A doctor is the President of Ahzar University. Yes, a doctor is now the President of Ahzar ash-Sharif; all of them they are doctors. From where is this title coming? Do you see it in the Holy Qur'an? Ignorant ones; no lights to see from where honor is coming to them. It is not coming through empty, imitation titles that they are imagining or they are making. They are making up titles, *istina'i*, imitation, not real ones. They are thinking that this title gives them something and running after such nonsensical titles. And they are ignorant.

Therefore, if I see at the beginning of his name "Doctor," I am saying "Leave him," never, never understanding the existence of the glory of the dominions of the Lord of the

Heavens, Allah Almighty. Leave that one; leave that one. Don't listen to him.

You can't learn anything from them, no. Common people may be ignorant and they may say, "Yes, I don't know. I am ignorant, I am not learned." But those who are saying, "We know because we are doctors," don't believe them. They are imitation ones. As a person, if claiming "I am a doctor" and using an imitation, false diploma, harms people, also if a person uses that empty, imitation title, if anyone listens to him, they are going to be more ignorant ones, because an ignorant person can teach people ignorance, nothing else. He is ignorant; what is he going to teach? Must teach ignorance. A [really] learned one may teach you something of knowledge, that knowledge that belongs to that glorious one, and his glory includes every divine attribute. Therefore, the rank of the Seal of Prophets ﷺ, no one can reach that point; no. And he is only one, also; can't be two.

May Allah forgive us. People, they are never running to learn the real, real points of Reality,[13] and that belongs to that reality, the glory of that glorious one. They are not understanding. And therefore people's level now is the lowest level.

Earlier, they were looking in order to understand something. Real researchers, they were running to know something, but now people they have been dressed in the gar-

---

[13]That is, the Reality that pertains not to this material world and its manifestations, but the higher Reality that was known and manifested through the Seal of the Prophets ﷺ.

ments of Shaytan's pride. That pride is making a barrier between themselves and Reality. And each time they are looking through that barrier and saying, "We are this!" Shaytan is cheating them through their egos and they are falling into darkness, into dark worlds.

Therefore, the levels of people now are the lowest, and every trouble is coming from that point. And people, they are in need to be saved, but those "doctors" are making them more ill. Instead of treating them, they are giving more trouble to them, harming them and making them to be in a *bahr-ul-hayreh*, the ocean of bewilderment and astonishment. They are saying, "What? Where?" falling into it, and they can't see, they can't get a feeling, and they are in fear and in a hopeless situation, and every trouble is just growing in that sphere.

May Allah change our lives from a dirty life to a clean life, and change His servants from putting on themselves imitation garments, and put on them real garments that shine and give glory to their wearers.

May Allah forgive me and bless you. For the honor of that most glorious one in His Divine Presence, Sayyidina Muhammad ﷺ —*Fateha.* ▲

3

A GIFT DEARER THAN GOLD

A'udhu bil-Lahi min ash-Shaytani-r-rajim. Bismillahi-r-Rahmani-r-Rahim. La haula wa la quwwata illa bil-Lahi-l-'Aliyyi-l-'Adhim. By the name of Allah Almighty, All-Merciful, Most Beneficent and Most Munificent.

Everything reaches to Allah, everyone reaches to Allah. Allah. He knows where everything is; He knows where everyone is.

Olden-time people, they were saying and we were believing, and also now we are believing, never changing that belief, that if no permission for a thing to move from its place or to change its position, it can't be without His order; there can't be any movement outside of His will. Everything must be by His will.

A leaf on a tree, those old people were believing, can't move if its Creator, its Lord, does not give permission to move. And no bird can open its wings to fly; without His permission, they can't open, can't fly. Everything is under such perfect control. And He is asking that people must know this, not to say, "I can go, I can come, I can do, I can not do" —no. Everything is just controlled.

Let alone the children of Adam, but an atom can't change its position without His command, without His permission, saying, "I am changing my position, O my Lord." Its desire and the divine will are coming [together] and changing its position to another way. *Subhanallah!* And that one, that atom—it is impossible to ask for changing its position by itself; that feeling must be granted to that one to ask. If Allah Almighty does not give that inspiration to that atom, it is impossible for it to ask for a change of its position by itself. *Allahu akbar!* That atom must ask and Allah must give.

He is not obliged to give, but His generosity towards all creation makes everything to ask because He is the Giving One for everything, for everyone. His generosity makes that atom to say, "O my Lord, I am asking to change my position." And that changing, it has a wisdom, it has a reason, it has some need so that that one is asking. But that inspiration must come to that atom, and the Lord is answering that one and giving that possibility, or giving that atom energy to use it for changing its position, because every movement needs energy. If not granted that energy, that atom can't move—can't move.

It is like a car without fuel. The car is ready, but if you do not put petrol in it, it can't move. That car needs power for running and therefore it is signaling to its owner, "Take me to the petrol station. I am finishing. Fill me with energy for movement." And that atom is calling and saying, "O my Lord, I am in need, from Your endless generosity, of support for energy or energetic support to continue Your glorifying."

From one position to another, another glorifying is coming, and glorifying is going on endlessly from every creation. From every smallest particle of creation, they are, they *must*, glorify their Lord. And they are asking, "O our Lord, from Your generosity, give me energy, give me support through Your divine Energy Oceans to continue glorifying You." *Subhanallah!* You can reach that point by thinking?

And He is asking from His creatures, common ones,[14] only glorifying, because their creation is not the same as the creation of mankind. Mankind's creation is just different, at the top level of creation. The highest limit of creation has been granted to mankind, and therefore Allah Almighty is putting mankind in such a position, giving them such value, and through that value granting them the garment of the honor of glorifying. And man's glorifying is at the highest level position.

Our body, each smallest unit of our bodies, glorifies, but the top glorifying that the Lord is asking from mankind and making mankind to be more pleased, that level is to say, by their own will, "*Subhanallah, subhanallah, subhanallah, al-'Aliyyi-l-'Adhim*"[15]—to use you will and to say "Glory be to Allah." Yes; that is the top point.

An unbeliever, his body is also glorifying, but that person is saying, "No God." Yet every part of his body is saying, "You are our Lord. Glory be to You, O our Lord!" But that foolish one, heedless one, is not saying it and is denying.

The top point of glorifying is when you say, "*Subhanallah.*" Therefore, we begin, after praying, to say, "*Subhanal-*

---

[14]That is, the levels of creation below mankind.

[15]*"Glory be to Allah, glory be to Allah, glory be to Allah, the Most High, the Almighty.*

lah, subhanallah, subhanallah, sub-hanallah . . ."[16] Out of His generosity, He is asking His servants to glorify Him, Almighty. And the glorifying of servants to their Lord makes them to come closer to His divine Generosity Oceans, to be granted more and more. That is the meaning of *"Hal jazau-l-ihsan illa-l-ihsan?"*[17] In proportion to their smallness, His servants are trying to give out of their generosity and to say, "Glory be to our Lord," and He is granting, *yukafiuhu,* rewarding, His servant.

Once a *badu,* a bedouin, was saying, "I must go to Baghdad."

Baghdad, Baghdad. Eh! They lost glorifying their Lord and every curse is coming on those people. Allah Almighty, in the Holy Qur'an, is teaching His servants. And what is He saying? *"Ya-ayyuha-l-ladhina amanu, la tarfa'u aswatakum fauqa sauti-n-nabiyi."*[18] O believers, don't raise your voices above the voice of My beloved Prophet. Let his voice be the loudest. Don't shout, don't shout! To be humble is your characteristic, O *mu'mins."*[19]

They are running. They are thinking that the Prophet ﷺ is not with them. *"Wa- 'alamu anna fikum Rasul-Allah."*[20] The

---

[16]According to the Prophet's practice and teaching, after finishing the formal prayer, Muslims are accustomed to saying, thirty-three times each,"*Subhanallah..., Alhamdulillah..., Allahu akbar* (Glory be to Allah..., Praise be to Allah..., Allah is Most Great)."

[17]*"Is the reward of good [anything] but good?"*(55:60)

[18]49:2.

[19]Believers.

[20]*"And know that the Messenger of Allah is among you."* (49:7)

Prophet ﷺ, he is not away from his nation. Allah is saying, "He is with you," not only with those who are sitting in front of him; that verse means with his whole *ummah*. Therefore, control you voices. Don't shout. Let Prophet's the voice be loudest. He may address your Lord on behalf of you.

What are they doing? In Islamic countries, people are running like foolish ones through the streets and shouting, shouting, saying, "Russia, down! America, down! England down!"—shouting and running. Why are you saying, shouting, this? Why are you not saying, "*Ya Rasul-Allah*, look after your *ummah*." Humbly go to mosques and say, "*Ya Rasul-Allah*, you can be in the Divine Presence because intercession has been granted to you. Please use your intercession for us, on our behalf, to be saved from the hands of those cruel people, from wolves, from foxes, from dragons. *Ya Rasul-Allah*, make your intercession for your nation!"

But they are not saying it, thousands of people running through the streets, shouting—not only men, but also women, to whom Allah Almighty is ordering, "*Wa qarna fi buyutikunna wa la tabarrajna tabarruja-l-jahiliyati-l-ula,*"[21] Allah ordering *mu'min* women to be in their homes, not to go out just to be seen. He is *yamna'*, prohibiting, them to go out of their homes, as the women of the time of Ignorance[22] used to do, running in the streets with their *zeenah*, orna-

---

[21]In this verse, addressed to the Prophet's wives in particular and to all Muslim women in general, Allah is ordering, *"And abide in your houses and do not display yourselves [in the manner of] the display of the former times of ignorance"* (33:33).

[22]*Jahiliyyah*, the period of ignorance of divine guidance mentioned in 33:33 above.

ments, to make men to look at them, Allah Almighty has prohibited that [to Muslim women]. [23] How are they running through the streets and shouting? And raising their voices to draw attention to themselves, that is wholly wrong, also.

What is happening in Islamic territories is because they are on the wrong way, men and women. They are running on the wrong way, and [because of that] wrong way, curses are coming on them, in Baghdad and other Islamic territories. No; it is not permitted for men and women to run through the streets and to shout—no. Muslims should only go to the mosque and cry and ask for intercession from the Prophet, to be intercessor in Divine Presence and to ask forgiveness, not in the streets. Wrong way, the Muslim world now! Therefore, curses are coming on them. They can't blame America, Russia, China, Turkey and other countries; no. The blame is on ignorant groups of Muslims, shouting in the streets, not going to mosques to ask forgiveness from Allah Almighty and His beloved one's intercession. *La haula wa la quwwata illa bil-Lahi-l-'Aliyyi-l-'Adhim!*

That person, that bedouin, he was living in the desert. One day he was saying to his wife. [Mimics:] "I would like, O my darling, to visit the *khalifa, Amiri-l-Mu'minin*.[24] O my darling, what do you say to this?"

She was saying, "As you like, my darling. You can go."

---

[23]That is, to be on public display and mix physically with men.
[24]The caliph, the Leader of the Believers.

"Yes, I can go, but you know that if we are going to visit *Amiri-l-Mu'minin*, I must not go without a gift in my hand. It is not good manners. I must take something to him."

They were thinking what they could send to the *khalifa*, *Amiri-l-Mu'minin*. Then they made their decision.

"O *habibiti*, my darling, fill that clay pot with water. We can take it because it is very valuable in our place. I must bring to him our most valuable gift in the desert. Nothing can be more valuable than a pot of water."

She said, "It is good, very good," and she filled it, and he took it and put it on his shoulder. Then he went to Baghdad and asked "Where is the *amir's*, our *sultan's*, palace?"

They said, "Here, there; here, there," and he found it. He arrived, and a guard was saying:

"Who are you?"

He was saying, "I am a bedouin, coming from desert, asking to meet *Amiri-l-Mu'minin*."

"Oh, you are asking to meet *Amiri-l-Mu'minin*?"

"Yes. I am a citizen of his nation, and I know that I have a right to meet my *sultan*."

Then the guards were looking at each other. "What shall we do?"

One was saying, "Sit down here. We may send to *Amiri-l-Mu'minin*, saying, 'Someone has come from among the bedouins and is asking to meet you. If you accept, we may let him come.' [To the bedouin:] If not, you can't go in."

They were sending someone. That one was running and coming, saying, "O *Amiri-l-Mu'minin*, one peasant, one bedouin, has just come and he is asking to meet you, to see you."

And *Amiri-l-Mu'minin* was saying, "Let him come."

And the guard came and gave good tidings. "Come, follow me, follow me, follow me," till reaching the hall of the throne.

Amiri-l-Mu'minin was sitting there. "Welcome!"

"O *Amiri-l-Mu'minin*, it came to my heart to visit *Amiri-l-Mu'minin*, and I am coming from a far place, from the desert. *Alhamdulillah*[25] that I am seeing your brilliant face, the Lord of the Heavens putting on you the brilliance of *iman*[26] and crowning you with His greatness, the crown of greatness making you on the line of the family of the Prophet 🌸. I am happy, I am thanking to Allah Almighty."

And these words were entering the heart of *Amiri-l-Mu'minin* and he was saying—the bedouin was carrying this pot on his shoulder—and he was saying, "Put your pot here. What is that?"

"O *Amiri-l-Mu'minin*, it is the Prophet's advice, if one person visits another, that he must bring something as a gift. If bringing nothing, if on the way he finds a nail, bring it and say, 'I have only this. Take this as my gift to you.' Therefore, from the *sunnah*,[27] the holy command of your

---

[25]Praise be to Allah.

[26]Faith.

[27]The practice of the Prophet 🌸.

aba', of your grandfather, *Paygamber*, from *Rasul-Allah, jad-dukumu-l-'ala*,[28] I am bringing to you a gift that is the most valuable gift anyone can bring to you."

And he was saying, "What it is in it?"

He was saying, "Water."

"Oh-h! May Allah bless you! The Lord of the Heavens is saying, *'Wa ja'alna mina-l-ma'i kulla shayin hayy.'*[29] You did your best for me, bringing me the cause of life. I am thankful to you, O my citizen, O 'Abdullah."[30]

Out of his good manners, he did not say that the Dijlah, the Tigris, runs through Baghdad and we are sitting by water. He said, "You did your best, you brought your best gift," and ordering his servants, "Take his gift. Fill my pots from it and fill it with gold"; because if someone gives you a gift, you must also, as far as it is possible, give something to him. And he was saying, "Fill it with gold and give it to him to go back."

That is a story, a historical story that happened. When we are telling a story, don't ask if it happened or not, but you must look at what is the wisdom in it. All tales give

---

[28]*Rasul-Allah:* the Messenger of Allah; *aba':* father, forefather, ancestor; *Paygamber:* prophet, the Prophet; *jaddukumu-l-'ala:* your illustrious ancestor.

[29]*"And We made every living thing from water."* (21:30)

[30]Here, the caliph is addressing this unknown citizen of his realms by the most honorific title, "'Abdullah," meaning "servant of Allah," as a sign of respect for his being a believer.

some lessons and teach mankind something, something to be more perfect.

Filling it with gold and giving it to him; he had brought his most valuable gift through the desert. "And we have treasures, and we are *muqabiluhu*, returning to him from our treasures." And when Allah Almighty is ordering to His servants to glorify Him, Almighty, He is not in need of your glorifying, not even going to be like water to *Amiri-l-Mu'minin*. And Allah Almighty, from His Glorifying Oceans, is dressing that one in a glorious garment whose price, value, no one can think of.

Therefore, our bodies, each part is glorifying, but heedless people are not using their tongues to say, "*Subhanallah, subhanallah, subhanallah.*" Shame on mankind that they are claiming they are civilized people! But they are not civilized because they do not know the rights of the Lord of the Heavens, to give Him their best grants, to glorify their Lord.

And till they are coming to that point, troubles are going to be never-ending. They will continue till not even one person remains on earth. It is enough; one man, one woman, it is enough. As He, Almighty, began the descendants of Adam from one man and woman, if even one man, one woman, remain, He may give new descendants whose importance is only to say, "*Subhanallahi-l-'Aliyyi-l-'Adhim, subhanallahi-l-'Aliyyi-l-'Adhim, subhanallah wa bi-hamdihi,*"[31] and to glorify their Lord with countless kinds of glorifying.

---

[31]"Glory be to Allah, the Most High, the Almighty" twice; "Glory be to Allah, and for Him is all praise" once.

That is the time that is coming, the time of Mahdi ﷺ, then Sayyidina 'Isa ﷺ.[32] Be awake! Beware of Shaytan! And wake up to catch the train before it runs away, getting in. Don't remain at the station, O man! We are addressing all mankind on earth, from East to West, West, from North to South.

May Allah bless you and forgive me. For the honor of most honored one in His Divine Presence, Sayyidina Muhammad ﷺ—*Fateha.* ▲

---

[32]Mahdi: the divinely-appointed leader whose coming is foretold in numerous *hadiths*. 'Isa: the prophet Jesus ﷺ, who, according Islamic belief, did not die but was raised alive to Allah and will return at the end-time of this world to rule mankind according to the *Shari'ah* (sacred Law) brought by Muhammad ﷺ.

4

SHAYTAN'S MISSION

A'udhu bil-Lahi min ash-Shaytani-r-rajim. Bismillahi-r-Rahmani-r-Rahim. La haula wa la quwwata illa bil-Lahi-l-'Aliyyi-l-'Adhim.

We are running from Shaytan to Allah. Shaytan is a dog, always running after mankind to bite them; never getting to be friendly with mankind, never going to be just to mankind, never going to be true with mankind, never going to make mankind happy, never going to make mankind be servants of their Lord. That is his mission. You *must* understand, all of us must understand, what is the mission of Shaytan.

His mission is trouble-making, and that trouble is for mankind. He is not going to make trouble with angels, no, because the Heavens are protecting the area of angels. It is impossible for Shaytan and his armies and helpers and supporters and agents to go up, to reach angels' level; he would be kicked out and thrown down. He does not even take too much care about animals, also, because animals are not carrying any responsibility.

His mission only is mankind, to take them away from servanthood. His mission is to give trouble to mankind. His mission is to destroy everything that mankind is doing and working on, asking to destroy it materially or spiritually; running after mankind, and whoever is following him must fall into endless troubles. As long as a person is following Shaytan and his ways, following his teachings, at every step, at least one trouble, and after that countless troubles, should surround him. Every trouble is bringing sufferings to mankind, and every trouble that mankind is falling into is because they are following Shaytan and his teachings, giving poison—giving poison, and the lives of people are becoming poisoned.

They are saying "air pollution". In so many countries people are putting something on their noses and mouths because the atmosphere is dirty, and more than dirty, poisoned. They are drinking, and poisoning their drinks, also. And everywhere that mankind is running, in every field, *majal*, that mankind is running after Shaytan, at every step they are going to find a trouble. And they are going to be surrounded by a poisoned atmosphere materially, and then that material poisoning will affect their personality, that personality that represents their spiritual being.

Our spiritual being is so nice, so handsome, so beautiful, but because of that poison, our personality is going to be changed to an ugly appearance. So many people now are coming to me and they are complaining—old ones and young ones, youngsters, men and women, boys or girls. New couples are coming; they were so lovely to each other for some days, for some months, and then they are coming, and saying, "O shaykh, what is your advice to me, because my husband doesn't love me now." And she looks like a moon, so beautiful, but she is complaining that her husband does not love her as before, saying to her, "I'm fed-up with you." And sometimes a wife is coming and saying, "I'm just fed-up with my husband. I would like to divorce."

I am saying, "Your husband is such a handsome person, a good one."

But she is objecting and saying, "But I can no longer carry him." That means their personalities are poisoned by the causes, by the reasons, that are surrounding their lives, and putting on the 'eye glasses' that Shaytan is using to make false [appearances] among people to make *fasad*, corruption.

Everywhere, now, it is their problem that they are not able to carry each other, the wife her husband and the husband his wife. Before, the love that people were running after was giving them some lights, and their faces were getting brighter day by day because they were doing their Lord's service, and every service dresses men or women in lights and beauty and familiarity. But now people. they are never interested in their Lord's servanthood, in heavenly service in the Divine Presence; they are never taking any care. Therefore, that s coming to them as a punishment, the wife looking at her husband and saying, "So ugly, repulsive" the husband looking at her, saying, "Such a dirty face," *astaghfirullah!*[33]

And trouble is growing among people, and people they are thinking that this crisis is growing because of economic aspects. That is not true! It is not a result of an economic crisis, no! But they are never speaking on that point that is the most important point—to say that because people are running away from their Lord's servanthood, they are going to dressed in ugliness, men and women. And they are coming and saying, "O shaykh, I think some people are doing

---

[33]I seek Allah's forgiveness.

black magic on me because my husband doesn't loves me as before." Or men are coming and saying, "Perhaps someone is doing black magic on me. My wife doesn't love me as before."

All of them are lies, imagination! They are not mentioning the most serious point that is giving that trouble to mankind, to say, "Because you are not taking care of the servanthood of your Lord, you are not going to dressed [in light and beauty]."[34] You are remaining only with your physical beauty, and physical beauty is going to be like plastic figures [mannequins] in *mağazins*, shops, *konfeksiyon*.[35]

They may put clothes on the figures of men and women, but it is nothing. No taste with that plastic body, never giving anything to them, men or women. But if a person lets himself or herself be dressed in heavenly beauty garments that are a result of blessings from Allah Almighty, they will never lose their familiarity up to the end. He may be eighty, ninety, a hundred and more, never changing because he is always dressed [in that lovely characteristic].

There is a [piece of] traditional knowledge, coming from the Prophet's heavenly knowledge, that says that if anyone wants to be seen, or to be dressed, with beauty on themselves, they must try to be awake at midnight and dawn time, because that is the time that lights brighten, coming and dressing people. Therefore, those who are praying midnight prayers and dawn prayers, they should be known by their faces, Allah giving to them a bright and fa-

---

[34]That is, in spiritual beauty and light.

[35]*Mağazin:* a large store; *konfeksiyon:* ready-made clothing shop.

miliar *üz*.[36] If anyone wishes, he or she may pray to their Lord because at that time Allah Almighty is sending angels with heavenly lights and heavenly dressings, to be dressed on His servants who are in His Divine Presence on earth, praying to their Lord and giving their high respect.

But people, they have lost it, and they are insisting on doing beautification on their faces or on their bodies. And they are spending, not millions but billions of dollars, billions of euros, to buy this small jar of cream, cosmetic, for making their faces good-looking.

I was in South Africa. I went to a warehouse, a warehouse so big that when I looked up, my turban was going down [at the back]—so high. And small trains were running in it to carry these cosmetics. To bring them, one, two, three, four, five, six, seven, eight, nine, twelve trucks were coming. As a ship comes to a port, they were coming to take these cosmetics. And they were saying, "You know one small jar, how much it is?"

"I don't know. Is it Turkish money?"

"No. *Their* money." They were saying, "Five dollars, the smallest one."

This building was full. I was saying, "They can buy all of Turkey with this warehouse and its contents, so many."

All for *what*? For ladies. Using this to make themselves young, till no teeth are left; they are buying, and young ones, also. They are not saying that Allah is giving to them beauty, but they are asking to use something to be more beautiful.

---

[36]Variant of the Turkish *yüz*, face.

Can't be! As long as men look at women, it takes away from that beauty, from their faces, from their bodies. The ones who are guarding their faces and their bodies, their bodies and faces are always fresh and smooth without using cosmetics.

They do not know the main, main source of beauty, from where it comes. They are saying, "Why do women put on a *chaddor*?"[37]

"To guard their beauty."[38] But no mind now, women! "Why are they putting this veil on their faces and guarding their beauty?" They [*hijab*-wearing women] are very clever ones. They do not waste their beauty because that looking is *haksız, haris*,[39] taking from your beauty. Therefore, old ladies, our mothers and grandmothers, they were keeping their faces and their bodies from being hurt by the gaze of men who were not *halal*[40] to them.

What are we saying? People are coming, falling into troubles for following Shaytan and shaytanic teachings are harming mankind spiritually and physically. Before, spirituality was protected, and when their physical being was protected, more happiness and beauty was coming to them. But now they are opening,[41] opening and showing, asking to

---

[37]*Hijab*, women's covering.

[38]Natural adornments.

[39]*Haksız*: wrong, unlawful, illicit. *Haris*: avid, eager, desirous, greedy.

[40]*Halal*: permissible, here referring to men other than those near relatives mentioned in Qur'an 24:31 who are permitted to see women in their homes without *hijab*.

[41]That is, opening their attractions to public view.

show their beauty, but it is never going to be successful, their beauty quickly going away.

Particularly women, when they are working with men, they are getting hurt and going to finish quickly. Their youth is quickly running away. If any women are working among men, men's looking is hurting them, and their beauty and their physical being is coming down, coming down, coming down. And so many women are coming and saying they are ill. And what is the illness? They are saying to me, "O shaykh, there is tumor, cancer."

I am saying, "How old is she?"

They are saying, "Twenty-five."

Oh! How can it be? Just going down, particularly those girls who are going to universities, always with each other,[42] touching. By the time they graduate, they are finishing also physically. Then their parents are coming to me, saying, "O shaykh, do something to marry our daughter."

I am saying, "How old is she?"

"Thirty years old."

"Oh!"

"Twenty-five years old. Twenty-seven years old."

"Why? They are beautiful ones. How did they delay?"

"Because they like studying, doing a Master's, becoming a doctor."

---

[42]That is, mixing freely with men.

34

You finished; you finished in the university. You finished—finished; the wrong way for mankind, because they are following shaytanic teachings. And now the Turkish Government, I heard this morning, they are making a new rule: to be like Europeans, men and women are going to be equal.

Yahu,[43] how are men and women going to be equal? If they are going to be equal, all of us must be women. *That* is equal. Allah created you man, created her woman. How are you claiming that men and women are equal? What is that foolishness?

Up to here, *wasal!*[44] People's minds, government's decisions, are making a rule to make women [and men equal]. What is that? Then I am saying to them, "If it is a new rule, you must give the same rights to women as you give to men."

"How it can be, O shaykh?"

"Must be one president, a man; one president, a woman. One prime minister, a man; one prime minister, a woman. Ministers, as many as there are from men must be from women. One assembly for men and one assembly for women. If you say saying something and women do not say so . . . [Chuckles]. If you say, "Today is a holiday," and women say, "No," which should it be? If equality brings such foolishness, for what are they causing *tahriq?*[45] You are asking to make *fitnah,* corruption!

---

[43]Turkish equivalent of "See here!" an expression of impatience.

[44]To curry favor or seek to gain access, in the context of the Turkish government's efforts to enter the European Union.

[45]Provocation, excitation, stimulation.

Why are you saying this? What is the benefit? What are you going to do? Who is going to be at home? "Both of you, you should be outside. How can it be? What is that foolishness? Up to today, Allah Almighty is saying, *"Ar-rijalu qawwamuna 'ala-n-nisa',"*[46] Allah saying that men are taking care of women because women are weak and men are created powerful. A man can protect his wife but a wife can't protect her husband. What is that foolishness? Up to today. they are making that trouble for nations. Then they are never going to be successful.

May Allah forgive me and bless you, and send us from among His powerful servants a powerful shepherd for the *ummah*,[47] to send them to the way of Paradise, to save them from the hands of devils. For the honor of most honored one in Divine Presence, Sayyidina Muhammad ﷺ—*Fateha.* ▲

---

[46]*"Men are the caretakers of women."* (4:34)

[47]Nation or community, here meaning the community of Muhammad ﷺ.

5

EMPLOYMENT PREVENTS FALLING INTO SHAYTAN'S HANDS

A'udhu bil-Lahi min ash-Shaytani-r-rajim. Bismillahi-r-Rahmani-r-Rahim. La haula wa la quwwata illa bil-Lahi-l-'Aliyyi-l-'Adhim.

Allah Almighty is teaching His servants what is good for them here and hereafter. And He is also warning His servants what is bad for them, what harms them here and hereafter.

He created some minerals that are good for the health of mankind. Some others are poisonous, and some are against poison, anti-poison. Also, among plants, there are some plants good for health and some poisoning the body. Animals, they know what is poison for them and what is good for them. Particularly sheep, they are guided to healthy grass, healthy plants, and they leave alone some of them and eat some of them, eating what is good for them. They are animals and they have no will power, but their Lord is sending them to such food, grass or plants, that is good for them. And they are surrendering themselves to their Creator and they are living in safety for their eating.

All of them are just created for mankind. And mankind, they have been granted two precious characteristics or two precious grants from Allah Almighty. One of them is their minds, and second, Allah granted to them will power, so that no creature around us can be like a man. Men, they have a special creation, a specialized creation, an honored creation, the most valuable creation on earth. Allah Almighty granted to them that characteristic through their creation and dressed them from His own attributes, will and mind, intellect.

If Allah Almighty had not sent prophets for teaching mankind, through their minds they might know what is good for them and what harms them. Yes. Mind and intellect, which are a big grant from Allah Almighty, shows mankind and teaches them—and they can test it, also— whether something is good for them or not.

It is okay; everyone may know it. Whoever has been granted a mind, they know through their minds or through their intellect, and through their knowledge that they may try, giving them so much good knowledge for safeguarding their descendants; because all obedience or all servanthood that we have been asked to keep depends on sound knowledge.

That sound knowledge shows a person how he may be healthy, because if a person loses his health, he can't do anything, can't work and can't pray, can't stand by his servanthood because he has lost his health. Patients, sick ones, they are occupied with their health and they are under big pressure. They can't move, can't do anything, can't stand up because they have lost their health.

Therefore, as all grandshaykhs[48] have said, and also my Grandshaykh was saying (now, also, I am hearing it from him), that the most important thing for mankind to learn and to keep and to act on, is knowledge for keeping their health. That is important, to keep their health, and therefore knowledge is going to be of two kinds: *'ilmu-l-abdan* and *'ilmu-l-adiyan.*[49] You understand? Two kinds of knowledge. One knowledge that is granted to mankind is how they can keep their health

For *dunya* and for *akhirah,*[50] you must be healthy. Maybe a young person gets a headache and falls down, and he was like giant but some pain comes in his stomach and he falls down. Another pain comes from the back, from every part of his body, making him to fall down, while earlier he was able push an animal and to make *it* fall down, but then finishing. When he has lost his health, he is going to be burden on himself and on others, also. Therefore, first of all we should try to teach people how they can keep their physical being healthy. If no health, he can't pray, he can't carry on his servanthood. Therefore, that is very important. The most important point for our lives is to keep our physical being healthy up to the end.

Every prophet just came to teach people—first of all to teach them that they are servants of the Lord of the Heavens, and secondly, they were calling mankind, their nations, to stand up to fulfill their servanthood toward their Lord, Almighty Allah. Then Allah Almighty is teaching all

---

[48]High level Muslim saints *(awliya)*. "Our Grandshaykh" refers to Shaykh 'Abdullah ad-Daghestani, Shaykh Nazim's shaykh and predecessor.

[49]Knowledge of bodies and knowledge of religions.

[50]This world and the Hereafter.

prophets and saints which thing keep their health, because first of all, for being a good servant, they must keep their health.

First, prophets taught them, through that *iman*, what is necessary for praying, and teaching them, establishing for them, according to the holy command of Allah Almighty, that this is *halal* and that is *haram*.[51]

Everything from *halal* and *haram* is for what? What is the benefit?

Allah puts a limit for His servants and says, "This is your limit. Beyond this limit, you are falling into *haram*." That *haram* is disturbing and destroying your physical being so that you are going to be unable to give real obedience and servanthood towards your Lord, Almighty Allah.

That grant that Allah Almighty granted to His servants is *'aql*, mind; they may know through their minds. And intellect, also—that comes with mind. Mind balances everything through intellect; intellect is a balance. Mind sends to, "See what it is," and intellect is saying whether it is good or bad.

It is so easy; but then, what is difficult? Allah Almighty granted to mankind will power, that only He is using. That is a divine *sifa*, attribute, that He granted to mankind. He does not force His servants, but He granted to them willpower, giving value to man. Animals do things by force, and if a person is forced to do something, not using his will

---

[51]Permissible, lawful, and prohibited, forbidden.

power, he quickly goes down to the level of animals,[52] and it is not an honor for mankind.

Our mind and intellect speak according to the holy command that He granted.[53] Allah Almighty granted a list, a program, of some actions or some things, and you may look at it and may understand this is good, that is no good. When it is apparent, don't wait for Allah Almighty to force you to do this or not to do, because the biggest grant that even angels were not granted is will power.

We have will power, and our honor is with will power. Allah Almighty is putting in front of you a list of good actions and harmful ones, useful or un-useful things. Useful is what is *halal*, good for you, for your physical being as well as for your spiritual being. This list is okay for you. Another list [of *haram* actions] or things indicates that this harms you here and hereafter, and makes you to be under the hegemony of your ego or to be Satan's donkey. And this is forbidden, so that everyone knows what is good for himself or bad for them.

Everyone knows that smoking is no good, leading to drugs. Everyone knows that drugs are killers, physically and spiritually. Everyone knows that drinking is terrible and that it destroys people physically and mentally. Everyone knows that adultery is a bad thing, destroying you physical and spiritually.

---

[52]That is, animals are constrained ("programmed"] to do instinctively due to the nature with which they are created, having neither will power nor choice.

[53]Meaning that our minds/intellect must necessarily agree with Allah's limits because their being for the benefit and well-being of mankind is so self-evidently.

So many things are contained in that list. The number of harmful things, harmful actions, is eight hundred. Eight hundred kinds of actions have been designated in the *Shari'ah*,[54] heavenly commands, as harming you here and hereafter—here, making your level to come down, and on Judgment Day, making your level to be at the lowest position. And there are another five hundred actions that, if you are able to do one of them or all of them, it gives to you benefit. As the Prophet ﷺ was saying, *"Al-halalu bayyanun wal-haramu bayyan*[55]—what is good for you is mentioned; everyone may know. What is bad for you, everyone knows also that they are harmful."

Allah Almighty is teaching His servants, because without that knowledge you aren't able to carry the honor of being servants, of divine service. Therefore, He is putting [those limits] and then giving will power to you. "O My servant, look! These five hundred kinds of actions give you honor and make you to approach to My Divine Presence. Use your will power to bring yourself closer to Me through these actions. And beware that eight hundred kinds of actions are carrying you away from My Divine Presence, taking you to the sphere of curses, always coming on you curses from the Heavens. Beware, O My servants!"

Now most people are not using their will power. Animals know what it is good for them, what harms them. But mankind they know what it is good for them or bad, but they are not using their will power to stop it and to send

---

[54]The sacred Law of Islam, derived from the Qur'an and the Prophet's *Sunnah* (practice).

[55]"The permissible is clear and the prohibited is clear."

their egos to do good things, and to keep themselves from bad things.

Then what is the benefit of having will power from Allah Almighty? You are going to be like a person who has a jet plane but never uses it. What is the benefit of having a plane if you do not use it, or if you have a car, a good car, but you do not use it? What is the benefit of a good car being in front of you home, even a Rolls Royce or Mercedes or other famous car—what is their benefit? Why are you putting it there? Use it!

[Parodies:] "I don't like to use it, I like sleeping better. Better to sleep."

"*Yahu*, take that car and go to look around everywhere!"

"No, I am here, drinking. I don't like to open my eyes."

"Oh! If you don't like to open you eyes, why did Allah Almighty give you eyes?

Look, any animal is saying like you. Animals want to sleep twenty-four hours." But the new generation they are saying, "We like to sleep," putting there, there, these injections. For what? "We like to sleep."

What is that? You have been created for sleeping? Animals they are not sleeping as you sleep. Your new generation they are sleeping twenty-four hours, or twenty hours, or eighteen hours or fifteen hours or twelve hours or ten hours. What is that, what is that? That is the degeneration of the generation. Degenerated generations now, they are asking to sleep. If they open their eyes, not opening them [to be awake], but eating something, then making an injection and asking [to sleep more]. That is the twenty-first century's civilization?

People are asking me to go and to be present in a conference in Athens. And they are saying that we are coming here to look for some *çare*, cure, for youngsters. When I was in America, New York, at the U.N. building, there were so many posters, "Save youngsters from drugs." To whom are you addressing this, "Save youngsters from drugs"—*how*? And now the whole world is working on it. The biggest business is the business of drugs, to make youngsters to be degenerated generations.

Even if youngsters do not use it, they are sleeping more than enough. The limit of sleep for an adult is eight hours. After eight hours, sleep does not give comfort to our bodies but makes them to be tired. Up to eight hours, sleep makes *rahat*, rest, resting our physical being up to eight hours, and after it unrest comes.

And everywhere now, even if they do not use [drugs and sleep too much], the new generation they don't like to work. They have left plants, they have left gardens [farms]. They are asking for a *wazifah;*[56] all youngsters are asking to be employed by the government, to sit in front of table. [Parodies:]

"Why you are coming here? Go away! Come tomorrow." "Bring your paper. Take it! I am busy now." Like this, they are asking to be paid and to sit down in their rooms at their tables!

---

[56]Salaried employment, eligible for a pension.

Even police people are sitting in their office. And in colonial times, we know that police were going around *devriye*, patrolling, on horses and with *tüfek*, guns. [Laughs.] Yes. They were going around patrolling and no one could be *cesur*, bold enough, to do anything wrong.

Here, this small house in front of the mosque, it was the police center for this area. Six or seven on their horses for this whole area, forty or fifty villages. You could open your doors and windows; no one could take anything, could be able to come and to harm people. Now they are sitting in the police station. For what, this? Police must keep control, not sit in front of their tables!

One of the *gümrük muhafaza*, customs officers, was saying to me that once the *kaymakam*,[57] the commissioner of the district, was coming and asking, "Where is the *çavuş*, sergeant?"

And they were saying, "He is on patrol."

And when he [the sergeant] came, that commissioner was asking, "Why do I not see you in front of your table?"

And he was saying, "O our commissioner, our table is on our horse. If we wait for people to come and complain, it is going to be worse and worse. We are running around, and bad-charactered people or the agents of Shaytan can't move. They know that we are on patrol, can't do anything."

Now the new generation is asking for *rahatlık*, a very restful life, behind their tables. [Parodies:] "Hallo, hallo! Yes, I am speaking from my desk."

---

[57]Governor of a district

[Underling, meekly:] "What shall I say?"

"Say that the director is in a meeting. It is I, I am the director. Who is that? Say to him that he is in meeting!"

"O my master, I said so, but he is saying this time is not the time of a meeting."

"Say that he has a meeting in the toilet, because the toilet is also a meeting hall. Say to him!"[58]

Making people *atalet*.[59] *Atalet* means that people want not to move, wanting everything to be brought to him and to enjoy himself. No other thought for them, only for their pleasures, not for helping people—no. For their pleasure they are doing everything. Therefore, people now are in the worst position.

Therefore I am going to speak to people [in Athens], *insha'Allah*, who are blaming poverty for making a crisis, saying, "After poverty, crisis; after poverty, wars; after poverty, fighting; after poverty, economic crisis; after poverty, that and this."

It is false. And Islam is saying, *"Al-kasibu habibu-Llah."*[60] *Harik yadaik!* After *harika, baraka*.[61] Islam is saying, "Make your hands to work because blessings will come on you." You must know that to move, to work, brings *baraka*, blessings.

---

[58] Shaykh is mimicking the supercilious manners of young, well-to-do, business people.

[59]Inertia, idleness, inactivity.

[60]"The one who earns is loved by Allah."

[61]"Move your hands! After moving [them], blessings."

Therefore, our people, our ancestors, they were rising before the sun shone. Those people now, youngsters, they are lying like a *timsah*, crocodile. It is sleeping, sometimes opening [an eye], looking; if something comes, running at it, eating and looking if anything else is coming. Becoming like crocodile, or scorpions [chuckles]. *A'udhu bil-Lahi min ash-Shaytani-r-rajim!*[62]

May Allah forgive me and bless you. Where is Islam, what is our situation now? We are Muslim people. I am sorry and in sadness that they want to follow Western people who like to sleep.

May Allah forgive us and send us Mahdi ﷺ, and Jesus Christ, 'Isa ﷺ. For the honor of the most honored one in His Divine Presence—*Fateha.* ▲

---

[62]"I seek refuge in Allah from Satan the cursed."

47

6

ADDRESSING A CONFERENCE OF
RELIGIOUS LEADERS

[Here, Shaykh Nazim reads from a prepared text, addressing the attendees at the Athens Conference of Religious Leaders.]

Bismillahi-r-Rahmani-r-Rahim. A declaration [statement] for a conference in Athens that deals with the increasingly bad world situation.

You can understand my English or not? Don't sleep, anyone!

This conference is a good sign that good feelings are still alive among people, while we are living such bad conditions. And these good feelings belong to the Heavens. I am happy for this because this is a sign that we can still hope to save mankind and that it is not wholly finished; no.

Anyone may see that day by day the situation is getting worse for mankind and that soon it will fall into a bottomless valley. What we are seeing is the degeneration of the children of Adam and Eve. Yet we can still find representatives of goodness and people possessing heavenly characteristics.

Through this conference, the will of these good ones is evident. They are concerned about the future of mankind; I am happy. But it is the biggest, heaviest and most difficult goal that mankind can set itself, because those good people attending such a conference are the weakest group among mankind. They are at the mercy of tyrants, and they come to this conference full with hope but also full with fear— fearful because fear holds power over all nations or covenants of mankind on this planet.

Enemies of mankind are monitoring what is happening through this meeting now. These enemies never like this world to be changed into another, more peaceful world, or for there to be a new covenant for the whole world. That is because they have arranged their lifestyle in order to benefit from the existing miserable, violent, unhappy conditions of modern life, and if anyone is there to try to change these conditions, millions of such a people will ask, "What are we going to do? How are we going to live?" With very strong force—crises, problems, poverty, cruelty and violence— quickly they will rise up and ask, "Why are you coming to stop our importance on earth?" such a point people. "Who gave you this authority and who will give power?" Don't you know that you are the weaker ones? It is we who hold power in our hands. Don't think that we will give way to you, and if you insist, we will get rid of you easily."

They can't do it; but they can't do it. They may claim such a thing, but we are powerful yet because we are with the Lord of the Heavens. However, among us here, there are politicians. Politicians, also, they are builders of this world's contract now. But some politicians are not happy with a new change to come on earth, and with their tricks and traps fill this world and prevent this new contract. And that's why I am seeing that this meeting has no power at all to change the course of events. Its situation resembles that of an ant that has been asked to carry a big truck. Can't! An ant can carry a truck? It is not possible; we are weak. If the ant is able to carry that truck, then a conference such as this and those attending it would actually be able to make a change beneficial to mankind.

I myself—I am speaking on myself, that I am going to be nothing. I myself, I am pushing ninety; therefore, I need two persons, taking me from this, two persons from that side; climbing towards ninety, and I see so many others here, our holy people, metropolitans,[63] bishops and archbishops, who are perhaps a little younger or older than me (I don't see any older than me here). And they are all thinking, "How long until we enter into the Divine Presence? We are coming near to our end, and we are asking for some young people to awaken and to distinguish between those who are against humanity and those who are helping to establish real humanity and peace, giving everyone their rights."

Another point that I would like to address to this honorable gathering of holy people and others, like my sons, daughters, or grandsons, granddaughters, all who believe, who belong to heavenly religions,[64] is this:

You all know what is written about the beginning of this world and about the first contract on earth; it is men-

---

[63]A primate of the Greek Orthodox Church.
[64]That is, Jews, Christians and Muslims.

tioned in the holy books.[65] That first covenant also entails believing that Adam was the first man and Eve the first woman. Even if universities are not accepting it, but they were not witnesses when mankind beginning. They are only saying "theory," the theory of Darwin that people are coming from apes.

I am not coming from apes. If he [Darwin] likes to come from apes, he may come! Who is accepting to come from apes? If you don't like apes, you can ask to be from the line of gorillas or chimpanzees, such [ones]. No! [Laughter.]

And about the first man and first woman that Allah created for Adam, they lived together in the heavenly Garden of Eden, and they were happy with their lives. According to the holy command of the Lord of the Heavens, their generations descendants spread out over the world. Eve always gave birth to twins, a boy and a girl, and they were given the divine order to marry the firstborn twin boy to the girl of the second couple of twins. But that one with whom mankind is mostly friendly to nowadays, the devil, Satan, looked at Cain, who then disobeyed the heavenly command and refused to give his sister to Abel. Satan said to him, "Don't accept this because your own twin sister is more beautiful, so don't give her to Abel." So Shaytan made Cain to kill his brother, and he became the first murderer, thereby causing Adam and Eve to fall into deep oceans of sorrow and misery, their life which was so sweet then becoming so bitter.

---

[65]The Old Testament and the Holy Qur'an.

Attendants of this conference, do you know this from your holy books or not? If you don't know it, then what you believe in?[66] As Christians, Jewish, Protestants, Catholics or Orthodox, you must know it. And we as Muslims also believe this. The first man fell into an endless ocean of misery and he tasted no more the good taste of life. It was finished for him. And from that day up to today, do you think that Satan has ever left mankind?

No one can stand up and object to what I am saying, as I am speaking from the reports of all holy books. Therefore, I don't believe what it is written about the aims of this conference. They propose to do something and they list some reasons for the terrible state of humanity, but they are never mentioned the name of Satan as the cause. They talk about the problems of technology, the fall of the Soviet Union, and they are saying that poverty is a problem, but all of this is of no relevance. Satan, the devil, is making people to be enemies to one another. But he is masked, so people never curse Satan. Instead, they take him as an advisor and friend.

This is the time of devils and evil, and the whole world is full of them. We must know whom we are fighting. If we are good and well-intentioned people, we must show others who our enemy is so the real enemy may be recognized. The Lord of the Heavens says Satan is your most dangerous enemy.[67]

---

[66]Meaning that this information must be believed because it is contained in the Old Testament. It is also partially found in Qur'an, 5:27-32, and elaborated on by the early Qur'anic commentators such as Ibn Kathir and al-Tabari.

[67]Qur'an 2:168, 208; 6:142; 7:22; 12:5; 17:53; 18:50; 20:117; 28:15; 35:6; 36:50; 43:62.

Try to know about him and to recognize him. Don't say technology, poverty, the Soviet Union breaking down. All of this and every movement against humanity has been woven by Satan and his followers. If we do not know against whom we are fighting, we will lose the battle and we are never going to be victorious.

O our valuable attenders, this conference is a good start and a sign that mankind is beginning to awaken. Even if so slowly, mankind is becoming fed-up of evil and devils, and beginning to stir. They want a change, and that is a good sign.

Throughout the history of mankind, as we learn it from the classical books and holy scriptures, these problems have never ceased. As long as Satan is at work, problems, sufferings and cruelty will never end.

The holy books say that people will never stop disagreeing. People are always fighting, bad ones against good ones. Sometimes the good ones reach to power but mostly the cruel ones take over. Nowadays on our planet, no one can say that good, heavenly people are ruling the world, so peace cannot be established.

So when can we expect that the world will be changed by a new contractt? Only when the good ones come to power, then we know that cruelty will go away and the whole world is going to be saved. Therefore, look at the signs of awakening that are appearing now. Through such a good conference, an awakening is coming to mankind now. They are drunk from devils and evil, but now gradually mankind is starting to ask, "Where are we now? What are we doing?" This is a sign that people are becoming sober.

That is my declaration. It's my belief that only a heavenly intervention can change the direction of people not to follow Shaytan but to follow heavenly commands. If they do not follow heavenly commands, it is impossible for this world to attain peace through our own ideas, conferences, or by any of our own efforts and means.

This is a *big* proposition, to change [the] whole world, and as it is so big, must be so big a person, big personality, may change it, as prophets. And our Christian brothers, they are expecting—as we are expecting, also—Jesus Christ's coming. Before his coming, this world is going to be in such a dirty and terrible and violent position that we can't see [how] it is going to finish.

Finally, I am saying I was once upon a time meeting, inviting me, Patriarchi Bartaloma in Constantinople. And he was sitting on his chair and he was saying, "O Shaykh Nazim, what do you think about these troubles that are everywhere burning every place—what do you think about [them]? Do you know any *tedavi*, treatment, for them?"

"O Your Holiness, I am going to ask you only one question."

"What is that?"

I am saying, "Do you know, have you heard, that Shaytan is tired, or retired?'

He was beginning smiling and laughing (he never smiled, [just] sitting there). "If you can say to me that Satan retired, I am saying, 'Finished.' But he is yet in his power, running after people, making everything [bad]."

Therefore, if you know when Shaytan is going to be tired—never tiring, also, night and day running after us—or retired (if retiring, perhaps his salary may be cut from the Heavens; he is saying, I am no more, I am not working')" Then, finished; we can be saved. But if not, we are waiting for an intervention from the Heavens, that Sayyidina 'Isa must come, Mahdi ﷺ ﷺ must come, as our Jewish brothers they are saying that *Masiha*, the Messiah, should come, all of them now looking up, how he is coming. (I am not knowing if he is coming by this missile, coming; missiles going up, not coming down, bringing people down.)

Thank you for your attention. [Applause.] ▲

7

SHAYTAN HAS BEEN FORGOTTEN

A'udhu bil-Lahi min ash-Shaytani-r-rajim. Bismillahi-r-Rahmani-r-Rahim. La haula wa la quwwata illa bil-Lahi-l-'Aliyyi-l-'Adhim.

It is an Association.[68] By the name of Allah we must begin. For every action, for every function, for every effort, for every work—all must be for Him. You must not work for yourself! When you are working for yourself, you are not going to be His servants. You have been created for His Almighty's service, nothing else.

Therefore, the most important point is *for whom* you are doing what you are doing. You must think about for whom you are living, for what or for whom you are working. Yes.

But ignorance is covering all mankind. They are wasting their precious and valuable works, their valuable existence—they are wasting them. Everyone must know for whom he is working or for what he is working. This is an important question—*for whom I am working, for whom I am living.* Everyone must learn and know it.

---

[68]The gathering and discourse of a shaykh *(sohbet)* with his *murids* (followers).

But this time is a strange time and people, they are drunk ones. A drunk person never thinks, can't think. A drunk person, he has lost his mind, he has lost his intellect, he has lost himself. He has lost himself concerning why I am in existence and why I am running to do something—*for what*? And everyone knows that he is going to die, to pass away.

If that is so clear, no need to teach people that there is death and everyone is going to die. No need for teaching because they are, each day, hearing, seeing someone's death—sometimes one person, sometimes a hundred persons, sometimes hundreds, sometimes thousands of people are passing away, sometimes millions of people are dying. That means disappearing, finished. They are finishing; no more are they going to be seen among their families, in their homes, among their people, among their nations. No more are they going to be seen, one or ten or a hundred or a thousand, disappearing. They were with us yesterday and today millions of people have just disappeared. Yes!

A drunk person never thinks. A drunk person can't think because he has lost his mind; he has lost, also, his balance. Therefore, a drunk person makes himself, in the name of pleasure, to never think or know about problems for himself, for his life, and he isn't able to think about all nations or the worldwide problems of mankind; he can't think about it because he has lost his mind, not knowing. Perhaps he can only crow like a cock. When he gets drunk, he begins to sound like a cock or to bark like a dog or to kick like a horse or to bite like a donkey or dirty himself like a jackal, rolling in a field of dirt for pigs and thinking that he is so happy and that he has reached pleasure.

That person has just left his human attributes that give mankind honor. By using alcoholic drinks, people are leaving the good attributes of mankind that make them on the level of humanity, and they are thinking that we have reached the top level of our pleasure and top level of our happiness. That is their mentality when they are drunk.

That means that whoever uses alcoholic drinks makes himself fall down to the level of different kinds of animals, and he is happy to be among those zoo-people, with every kind of animal living there. And that person, by his will, by drinking and becoming drunk, thinks that he has reached the top point of pleasure.

Pleasure is something that can be tasted by a perfect-minded person. But if a person has lost that perfection, how can he be able to say, "I enjoyed"; never enjoying, because enjoyment is something that can be tasted through our minds and mental faculties? How can a person drinking and losing his intellect, losing the balance of his actions, losing everything that he knew before and becoming an empty-headed person, say, "I reached the top point of pleasure during my life by using drinks"? That is an ignorant one, and he is falling into the darkness of ignorance.

We are coming to the point now. Because the twenty-first century's people are thinking wrong, their ways are wrong, their direction of movement is wrong. Therefore, we are speaking on that important point, to prevent people from moving in the wrong direction.

What is the true direction, what is the right direction, and what is real pleasure? To be from mankind, not to be from the world of animals—to know this. We are moving in that direction because people they are drunk now, and drunk ones can't know anything. Therefore, to use drinks that are taking away the minds of mankind and destroying their good will, and making them forget or not use their intellect, those drinks are forbidden by all prophets. People who are running after their egotistical or physical desires that are represented by their egos, they are fighting against the rules that have been put in front of them by the Heavens. They are wholly denying the rules that are preventing them from following their egos, because anyone following his ego will never reach the right point in their lives, and they can't have enjoyment here or hereafter. Yes, Islam is saying so.

People are afraid of the name of Islam, and it is five letters, "I-s-l-a-m". Five letters are threatening Shaytan and his followers. They are trembling when they hear it; they can't even hear the name of Islam because Islam is the biggest barrier among those people from falling into Hells here and hereafter, saying, "Wrong way! Stop and go back!"

They never happy with Islam, although Islam never harms them. Do you think that Islam has harmed anyone except dragons? Islam is only against Shaytan and his representatives. Islam is only against the followers of the wrong way; Islam is only against satanic teachings; Islam is only against bad actions; Islam is only against cruelty; Islam is only against ignorance; Islam is only against adultery; Islam is only against bad actions that lead people to fall into endless Trouble Oceans, endless Suffering Oceans, and that want to prevent mankind from being in safety through Islam. But I am sorry to say that so many hundreds and thousands of scientists or academicians, or thousands of doctors who are claiming to be doctors of religion—I am sorry to say that those, even those people, are against I-s-l-a-m, against Islam.

Why? What has Islam brought to mankind? Where has Islam failed? Throughout fifteen centuries, where has Islam failed? Which rule of Islam is against humanity, while beyond Islam, everything is against humanity? But they are following Shaytan and they are trembling when they hear the name of Islam.

Don't fear it! You must fear Shaytan and his followers. Last week I was invited to a conference in Greece, Athens, and so many religious people were coming and attending. They were complaining, or, more than complaining, they were hopeless and full of fear for the future of mankind. They were addressing the attendees about what they were thinking, and I was listening to them. And they gave a short time for me, also, for addressing [the gathering]. But I used heavy bombarding for them; even one word was enough for them.

They said like this, like that. "I am sorry," I said, "that during the three days I was here I never heard, even from religious people, let alone others, philosophers or professors or teachers or representatives of so many foundations—I am sorry to say that even religious people, they never spoke, they never mentioned the name of Satan. No one, also, cursed him. I am sorry, because you have arranged your beliefs according to satanic teachings. You have taken the essence out of your religions and you are dealing with outward actions, and without essence, it is like a person without a soul. What benefit can you take from that dead body?

"Here, even, so many bishops, archbishops and professors are coming and speaking. Why are you not accusing Shaytan, why are you not accusing shaytanic teachings? Have you looked and do you know, from your holy books, that Shaytan is innocent, or are you looking and seeing, in every holy book that you have, that Shaytan is cursed by the Heavens? Why are you not saying so?

"Every trouble is from Shaytan because he was the first troublemaker, and he continues. And you are supporting his way, you are supporting satanic teachings, and then you are asking for a way to save people from sufferings and from violence, from war, fighting!

"You are asking [for such a way]. No, you can't find it. You must come to what the Lord of the Heavens is sending to you. That is Islam. You must say "Yes!" to Islam. As long as you are not saying "Yes!" to Islam, sufferings can't be ended and miseries are never going to be finished, and violence is going to increase, not to decrease, and wars and fighting are never going to be ended."

What shall we say? People, they are saying, "Oh-h, Shaytan, our best friend! How are we going to curse him? We have reached the top of civilization through our best friend, Shaytan," and you know, you see, to where the shaytanic teachings are bringing people now." Therefore we are saying, "Finished!"

You must learn first, mankind, for whom you have been created and for whom you have been offered to work, even when you are eating. That is a work and must be for a purpose. If you are walking, running, doing, everything must be for a purpose, and beyond purpose, there must be a wisdom, to be well-known. *What are you doing?*

One of our brothers was saying to me yesterday when I was coming to the airport, "*Subhanallah*, glory be to Allah!" That night they were showing a movie on TV in which some people were with Americans, some others against Americans, and they were fighting and fighting so that no one remained from both sides. And he was saying to me, "O shaykh, what you said during the daytime, that movie is making a *tasdiq*, confirmation, of your words." Just that night; yes.

What we are saying, it is not from, on behalf of me, but it is on behalf of saints and prophets, whom Allah Almighty is ordering to save His servants, to show them the true way for their lives. But people are running away. And as they are running, they showed that movie that night.

That is a wisdom from Allah Almighty, also, to see that, finally, people are going to destroy themselves by themselves. And that is the main goal of Shaytan, to destroy humanity on earth and to destroy every good thing that has been built for humanity—to destroy them and then not to remain even one man on earth, so that earth should be, when some nations are going to take away some others, empty, this world, the globe, going to be empty.

They [the attendees at the conference] are asking for a global change, but Shaytan is unhappy because he wants that global hegemony for himself. Therefore, he is trying to finish mankind on earth and then to be on earth as he was dreaming and thinking—to be *khalifs*. To be the deputies of Allah Almighty on earth, he is trying to take away all mankind, no one living on it. Then he will say, "Now we [he and his followers] are deputies on earth, now it is for us! This globe belongs to us. Oh-h, we took our revenge on mankind and mankind is just finished. Oh, hip-hip-hooray!" Shaytan is going to say to his followers, to his descendants, "Now the whole world is for us. We are deputies. Mankind is just finished." *Astaghfirullah al-'Adhim, astaghfirullah al-'Adhim, astaghfirullah al-'Adhim!*[69]

But Allah Almighty's divine order is to take away everyone who follows Shaytan and shaytanic groups, and to leave only His servants. Noah, when he was ordered to make that Ark and to put the believers in it, they were only eighty or ninety people; all others were killed in the flood. Satan was so happy that mankind was finished, but the Lord of the Heavens was saying, "I am not finishing them. What I said, that is reality and true.[70] I am not giving you that chance, O Shaytan and your descendants. I said that I am giving that honor to mankind only, not to you and your descendants. You are very happy that I made a flood and killed everyone, but I am leaving some people as a 'yeast' for mankind.[71] Among eighty or ninety ones, I am bringing back deputies. They should be My Prophet's followers and they should be deputies on earth. I am not giving that to you!"

And now there is coming another flood in which mankind are going to kill each other, killing, killing, killing. There should only remain a handful of people, but finally

---

[69]"I seek forgiveness from the Almighty."

[70]38:84.

[71]It is mentioned in a tradition from Ibn 'Abbas, the Prophet's eminent Companion and cousin, who had been granted understanding of the meanings of the Qur'an, that there were eighty people in the Ark.

Shaytan isn't going to be happy because Allah Almighty will give power for everything on earth to that handful of people from the nation of Muhammad ☿, bad ones going, and Shaytan is also going to be retired, changed and sent away. We should be *warithun*, inheritors, of this world, and on earth should be the flags of *"La ilaha illa-Lah, Muhammadu Rasul Allah ☿."*

May Allah forgive us and bless you. And we are asking to reach to those good days, by the honor of most honored one in His Divine Presence, Sayyidina Muhammad ☿— *Fateha.* ▲

8

"LORDSHIP IS MINE!"

A'udhu bil-Lahi min ash-Shaytani-r-rajim. Bismillahi-r-Rahmani-r-Rahim. La haula wa la quwwata illa bil-Lahi-l-'Aliyyi-l-'Adhim. By the name of Allah, Almighty, All-Merciful, Most Beneficent and Most Munificent.

Everyone must know of what he is need. If a person gets out and goes to market, and he does not know for what he went to the market, what will happen? What benefits can he reach, particularly if he is going from one distant place to another, coming from Glasgow to London, or from Belfast to Sheffield, or from Birmingham to Bury, or from Bury going to Dover, or from England to America? If he does not know for what he is going, what will happen? He will say, "Oh, for what am I coming here?"

And you—you are traveling from the Heavens. From the spiritual world, you have traveled towards the earth. That means that your real being is with your Lord in the Heavens; then you were sent to earth. If you don't know or if you are not asking for what purpose I have been [sent] to the earth, it is not like going from here in Lefke[72] from your home to market, or to Nicosia. or from one continent to an-

---

other continent, but you are coming, traveling on a journey from the Heavens to the earth, and you have been dressed in a garment that is not used in the Heavens—no.[73]

It is an important point, this Association. We don't know, and we are in need of someone to teach us and of learning the real reason of our traveling from the spiritual world and landing in the material world. The structure of the inhabitants of the Heavens is not the same as the structure of man on earth; this man on earth is not like that man in the Heavens, no. And—Allah-Allah, *subhanallah!*—the Lord of the Heavens brought the first man, Adam, from the spiritual world into existence in the material world. Therefore, the Lord of the Heavens used four elements—fire, air, earth and water, making his creation by His divine Hands, preparing, creating, then dressing his spiritual being.

That shape was just dressed for Adam's spiritual being, and that being was his real existence or real being or real station. Yes. And when the Lord of the Heavens sent that secret, real position of Adam's real structure in the spiritual world to come into [his physical form], He ordered Adam to get into relationship—his spiritual being to come and to make a relationship with that shape, with that new form that Allah Almighty had made and prepared to be the new manifestation of Adam's soul. Yes! And the Lord of the Heavens put him in Eden, *Jannati Adnin*,[74] to be there and freely enjoy himself with everything in the paradise of Eden.

---

[73]That is, the garment of materiality.
[74]The Garden of Eden.

Then the Lord of the Heavens, who is the Lord of all creation, the Lord of every creature, in order to make Adam and Eve, and after them their descendants, know that they all belong to the Lord of the Heavens, to make them to know that even though they are the top level of creation, they may still reach more and more levels . . . Do you think that a person, if he has power to reach the skies, do you think that anyone can pass that sky, the sky going under him and he is going above the sky? No, no! It is impossible; it is impossible. You can run everywhere on earth and you can test yourself by using so many nonsensical instruments to go up and pass through that space and reach the limits of that space, but it is impossible, Allah Almighty teaching them what is possible and what is not possible, what is *im*-possible.

And the Lord of the Heavens, the Lord of Adam and Eve and their descendants, wanted mankind to know that there is One, and that only that One has Lordship over everything. You—your level is servanthood, and there is no level for Him but He has Lordship over all creation, from pre-eternity up to post-eternity. His Lordship is permanent; no one can reach that point. Therefore, He ordered, "I am the Lord of the Heavens. I am the Lord of paradises. O Adam, I am your Lord and I am giving to you this Eden, Paradise, to live here and to enjoy yourself with everything. But I want to teach you that I am the Lord of you and your descendants. And as the Lord of the Heavens, I am saying, 'Don't eat, don't go near that tree.'"

O-oh-h! Therefore, the Prophet ﷺ , when sending his holy statement to kings and emperors, was saying, "I am Muhammad ﷺ , the messenger of the Heavens, who belongs to the Lord of the Heavens. I am calling you to follow me and to accept what I am calling you to—*that* direction. *Aslim taslim*, surrender. You should be in safety forever.

[Allah says:] "I am dressing you as an emperor or a king, but you can never pass the level of servanthood. I am the Lord. Prostrate to Me! I may give you safety here and hereafter. You must know that Satan, that cursed one, was struggling, arguing, with Me. He did not ask why Adam was at that station, but his accursed ego was demanding to be like Me.

"That accursed one, he was asking Lordship to be for him, also. Can't be! I am the Lord, One. All of you are My servants. Therefore I cursed him and kicked him out." And He was saying to Adam, "Don't be like that accursed one, to break My orders, and whoever breaks My orders, he is claiming to be the Lord like Me. I am not giving any way to anyone. This is eternal, eternal Lordship. From pre-eternity up to post-eternity, it belongs to Me, only to One! You must understand. Therefore I am putting this tree. Don't eat! I am commanding, and you are My servant and you must keep My orders, My commands."

Oh-h-h, *ya Rabbi! Tauba, ya Rabbi; tauba, ya Rabbi; tauba, astagfirullah!*[75] The twenty-first century's people, all of them are asking to be Lord, to have lordship. And some heedless ones, like Pharaoh, like Nimrod[76]—now countless Nimrods are claiming that they are lords, and that is the source of

---

[75]"Oh-h-h, O my Lord. I repent, O Lord; I repent, O Lord; I repent and seek Allah's forgiveness."

[76]The story of Pharaoh's oppression of the Israelites is mentioned in numerous passages of the Qur'an: 7:103-137, 20:42-73, 25:35-68, 28:2-42, 40:23-29,43:46-56, while Nimrod's highhandedness and tyranny are described in 2:258.

troubles on earth now, because they are not accepting the Lord of the Heavens and His commands. They are saying, "We don't care about that one's or anyone's orders. [Parodies:] "We are bringing democracy. Heh-heh-heh!" Killing people, voting, elections in Cyprus, elections in England, elections in America, elections in Russia. They are running to reach lordship over mankind. Yes? And the twenty-first century's people, each one is running to reach the station of Nimrod. Therefore Satan is urging youngsters, saying, "You must study."

"From where are you coming?" So many mindless youngsters, everywhere! You may ask, "From where?"

"I am coming from that place, Anta Maraş, or from Syria or from Egypt," even coming from Pakistan.

People, they are keenly wanting to reach a Master's degree or doctorate so that they may think, "A-hah!" Now, the last point for a person to reach is to be a doctor. Doctor Zumrud Husain, Doctor Iftikhar Husain, Doctor Fatima Begum, Doctor Zuhur-ul-Fatima, Doctor Amina Begum, Doctor No-Mind Begum. Ha-hah, everyone; making them to run after universities where Satan has put his *karargâh*, camps.

In all universities you may find them; they are all Satan's camps, *karargâh*. I am looking and seeing that they are just put on the *direk*, pole, post, of Satan, and he is preventing there to be, among the teachings of universities, any heavenly teachings. It is forbidden. No one among professors may speak about Allah or the Lordship of Allah or the commands of the Heavens or anything that belongs to the Lord of the Heavens. And that is the trouble.

And the Prophet ﷺ is saying, "Come, surrender to your Lord's commands! You should be in safety here and hereafter." Otherwise, some of you are going to eat some others till you are finished. As some of the Children of Israel killed some others,[77] now the whole world's people are going to kill each other till millions pass away, and a handful of people is going to remain on earth who accept the Lordship of their Lord on earth, in the Heavens.

May Allah forgive me and give us a good understanding. For the honor of the most honored one in His Divine Presence, Sayyidina Muhammad ﷺ — *Fateha.* ▲

---

[77]Referring to God's command to the Israelites who had not worshipped the Golden Calf to fight to the death those who had engaged in the sin of idolatry, as mentioned in 2:54.

9

THE BIGGEST SIN IS TO KILL

A'udhu bil-Lahi min ash-Shaytani-r-rajim. Bismillahi-r-Rahmani-r-Rahim. La haula wa la quwwata illa bil-Lahi-l-'Aliyyi-l-'Adhim. By the name of Allah, All Mighty, All Merciful, Most Beneficent and Most Munificent.

Every problem, every trouble, makes Satan happy. His first aim or his main goal is not to let the children of Adam be happy, either here or hereafter. He is thinking about nothing else. He is the first trouble-maker. His title in the Heavens is "the first trouble-maker," the first rebellious one in the Divine Presence, the first one who rejected the Lord's order in the Divine Presence.

And he was also giving his oath in the Divine Presence, addressing the Lord of the Heavens and saying, "You are making me to be cursed for the sake of that Adam and his children, and I am also swearing that I shall try to make them be cursed, not to be obedient ones to You. I shall give up my whole chance [for Paradise], up to the Day of Resurrection, for this. I am going to use it, and I swear by it that I am never going to give a chance to them to follow Your orders, so that all of them may be, like me, rebellious and disobedient and disrespected ones in Your heavenly kingdom.

"You should find them always not respecting You, Your heavenly sultanate. And I am going to give up my whole chance for that. I shall try to establish my kingdom on earth and I shall try to take away Your kingdom, Your sultanate, so that You are not going to find many obedient ones, only a few, and the majority should follow me."[78]

Yes. That is what he was saying, such dirty words in the Divine Presence, and when he was speaking in such a way, arguing in the Divine Presence, Allah Almighty ordered him to be changed according to his bad intentions and he was kicked out "Take away from him his [excellent] outward appearance, not to be as before when he was Azazil" (his name had been Azazil). "I granted to him honor and respect through his name and through his self, also, but, according to his bad intentions and bad actions, he has gone over his limit in My Divine Presence.

"I have changed his name from Azazil to Iblis[79] because he is never going to hope for My blessings, ever, changing his name from Azazil to Iblis and Shaytan. And his external appearance was so beautiful, so handsome. I granted that to him, but when he argued in My Divine Presence and changed his intentions, his nature, his natural being just became dirty, the dirtiest nature, and therefore I also changed his beauty into ugliness, to make his outward appearance the worst-looking, most violent—the most violent appearance for him, so that it may be seen that My curse has fallen on him."

And Allah Almighty said, "Demon, go away from My Divine Presence!" and he was sent out and ran away. He

---

[78]The story of Adam and Satan's rebellion is told in Qur'an, 2:35-39, 4:117-121, 7:11-25, 15:28-43, 17:61-65, 18:50, 20:115-126, 38:71-85.

[79]Meaning "one who despairs."

ran away because he had also been granted to be free for doing what his natural being wanted; it was a grant from Allah Almighty for him to do. He was free, and he has been permitted to go through East and West, from North to South. Throughout continents, among mankind wherever they may be, he can be there.

And he first began to do what he had given his oath about, beginning from Adam and Eve. And he was saying, "O Adam, I shall not leave you in Paradise. I was thrown out of your Lord's Divine Presence and I give my oath that I will not leave you to be in Paradise. Beware!" he was saying, also.

First, Allah Almighty was saying, "O Adam, beware of Satan! Try to protect yourself from him. Beware!" And Adam forgot for one second; for only one second he forgot his Lord's warning. And in that second, he did what Satan was asking him to do. That second, that gave a chance to Satan to be able to do his worst to Adam.

And in that second, Adam *asa Rabuhu fa-ghawa*.[80] In that second that Adam was disobedient, he forgot his Lord's command and then, in that second, he was a disobedient servant. He had been given a declaration in the Heavens,[81] but he forgot his Lord's warning and fell into the trap of his enemy, the trap of his enemy catching him so that he was then a disobedient servant.

---

[80]And Adam *"disobeyed his Lord and went astray."* (20:121)

[81]Referring to Allah's saying, *"O Adam, this [Satan] is an enemy to you and to your wife, so let him not drive you both out of the Garden so that you suffer."* (20:117)

"Take him out! My territory is only for clean ones, only for obedient ones. Disobedient servants can't be here; it is not the place for disobedient servants, it is not the place of disobedience. Take him out, him and his wife, also—out! Land him and his wife on earth, to be imprisoned on earth up to the Day of Resurrection. And let them fight with Satan on earth, he and his wife and their descendants; let them fight Satan and save themselves. Those who are obedient to Me, I am choosing them for My Paradise. Those who are not listening and obeying My Divine order, I am leaving them to be with Satan in the prison of Hells."

And up to today, in everything happening on earth, Satan is trying to make tricks for mankind and to put traps. Tricks are to make them step on, as a person steps on a mine. By his tricks, either a person may put his feet on it and—*woo-oo!*—going, suddenly finishing, and Satan is so happy; or making traps, not to kill and be thrown away, but like a trap that people put to catch some prey. And everywhere Satan is putting traps and making tricks.

And now in the twenty-first century, the whole world is full of satanic tricks and traps—*full!* And no one is warning mankind. Beginning from religious people, no one is writing on the walls of churches or mosques or synagogues, "Beware of Shaytan!" They are writing the names of cathedrals; they have a wooden sign, written on it "Saint George's Church," and writing under it. "This, that, this, that is going to be on Sunday, on Monday," but never writing on it, "Beware of Shaytan! O people, don't follow Shaytan! Come to be your Lord's servant. Don't pass by the cathedral without entering it. Don't pass mosques without entering them. Beware of Shaytan! Shaytan is preventing

you from coming inside them, inside mosques, inside cathedrals, inside synagogues. Beware of Satan!" No; and in East
and West, if anyone has seen [such as warning sign], let me
know.

Satan is putting his full hegemony on the whole world
now, throughout East and West; and no one is saying his
name, also; no. And mankind is so friendly to Satan, so
friendly. Everyone is happy with him and saying, "Our
best friend."

Your best friend is taking you to Hells! As a butcher leads
a sheep behind him to the slaughterhouse, mankind is running after Shaytan as sheep run after a butcher.

How are you going to find peace on earth? Each day,
every kind of criminals that Allah Almighty does not like is
making men harm each other. Daily they are showing so
many dirty photographs of the criminal actions that man is
doing to man.

It is not the honor of man to kill. Allah Almighty ordered His prophets to call people and to say to them, "O
people, come! I am calling you to make man *live*. Give life,
but don't take life."[82] The biggest sin is to kill someone
without a reason,[83] and Islam is ordering not to kill, not to
destroy.[84] Christianity, also, and Judaism, also; but
throughout the thousands of years up to today, you may see
that everywhere people are running to kill, to destroy, not to
let people rest.

---

[82] 5:32.

[83] 17:33, 25:68, 4:92-93.

[84] 2:190; 4:75, 92; 5:32/35, 6:151.

And Allah Almighty is saying, "*Yawma tati-s-sama'u bi-dukhanin mubin, yaghsha-n-nasa,*"[85] a Qur'anic verse in which Allah Almighty is threatening the people of the Last Days [of this world], on whom will come a smoke, making people to be like *sakran*, drunk, and they will not know what they are doing.

This [unseen] smoke has now arrived on earth before another smoke comes that you *can* see, but *this* you can only understand through your good feelings, through your conscience, that the whole world is veiled or covered, people wanting to kill, to burn, to destroy, not to be in peace. And fear has just covered the whole world like a smoke, and hopelessness, also, no one hoping to live. The feeling of hope has changed to hopelessness. No one can know if they will live up to evening, or from evening up to morning; they do not know. Fear and hopelessness have just covered the whole world.

May Allah Almighty forgive me and send us someone to change our lives and to save people from the successors of Shaytan and his agents, from devils and from evil. For the honor most honored one in His Divine Presence, Sayyidina Muhammad ﷺ— Fateha. ▲

---

[85] "*[Then await] a day when the sky will bring forth a visible smoke, covering the people. . .*" (44:10)

76

10

THE ONLY STATION IS SERVANTHOOD

A'udhu bil-Lahi min ash-Shaytani-r-rajim. Bismillahi-r-Rahmani-r-Rahim. La haula wa la quwwata illa bil-Lahi-l-'Aliyyi-l-'Adhim. Al-din an-nasiha.[86] By the name of Allah Almighty, All Merciful, Most Beneficent and Most Munificent.

Dün başka, bügün başka dır.[87] You can't find anything in a second or less than a second of time that is second or third or fourth or fifth or sixth or seventh or eighth or ninth or tenth—you can't find an end if you are going to divide a unit of time. And no one can say that time, it is something that is never-ending or without beginning—*azal, abadi.*[88] But the Creator just granted to His servants everything prepared in this world according to our capacity, because this world that mankind landed on and then their descendants spread on it, is only maybe like an atom in this well-seen universe, no more.

Beside the hugeness of the universe, our planet may be less than an atom. And on it we are living, millions or billions of people, and our physical beings, the space they oc-

---

[86] " The religion [Islam] is good advice." *(Hadith)*

[87] "Yesterday was one thing, today is another."

[88] Without beginning, without end.

cupy, *hajam*,[89] on this planet, it is also like an atom. It is so big for our [collective] size; this planet is so big. And then men, who have been landed on this planet, they have been granted some special and secret things by our Creator. Even though we are so small physically, that secret attribute that we have been granted makes us as though we are collecting within ourselves the whole of this planet.

And we are saying, "It is so small a world." Now people are saying it is so small, little globe, and now they are asking to look at other planets, to reach there. It is so small for us.

What do you mean to say by this? It is something important; yes. *Meded!*[90]

We have been granted to be on this globe and we have been landed, we have come into existence, on this planet. And the Lord of the Heavens, the Creator of this universe with countless galaxies, is saying, "*Wa wad'a-l-mizan.*"[91]

He put a balance. Nothing is without balance on this planet. That must be well-known. Everything is in balance, and that balance is for what? To show mankind that everything around them has just been put in a special way and has a balance.

You may look and see a tree, with branches, with leaves, with flowers, with fruits. And we are saying that it is a natural system that this tree is going to be like this or like that, growing from the right hand or growing from the

---

[89]Bulk, size, volume.

[90]Help, aid, assistance, support, backing.

[91]*"And He established the Balance."* (55:7)

left hand, or growing up or growing down towards the earth. We think that without balance that tree is growing, and its branches and leaves are coming without any balance, but it can't be. Every tree that grows must be under a balance, a Divine Rule:[92] up to where it is going to rise, where it is going to be with its branches, with which branch it begins, from where it begins, in which direction it is going to grow. And then that branch is also going to bring so many smaller branches, and at the end of those branches, leaves: at which point they are going to appear, then with which measure and balance the leaves are going to be arranged, when its flowers are going to appear, and then how its fruits should be. Everything must be in that balance.

You must use your mind to think about it. And by thinking about creatures, you may find a way to the Lord of creation, to the Lord of the Heavens. But it is important that, on this small planet that we are living with this nature, everything is just arranged according to our understanding level.

Then we are asking, "This planet, to whom does it belong?" A rule can't be without a ruler. We do not put the rules in nature, but we find hundreds and thousands of rules in nature. Who is that One that is putting those rules on this planet? Then you are asking for a way to understand, you are asking about the Creator, you are asking about the Arranger, Manifestor, *Mubdi*, and Creator. Who is that One? You are asking, and it is right to ask, also.

---

[92]A divinely established blueprint, so to speak, by which no part of the tree can deviate from the limits set for it or produce anything other than has been ordained for it or its kind.

Whatever understanding you may be granted, don't think that you are able to be granted a *whole* understanding. No; you can't carry that. That understanding concerning the Manifestor and Designer and Creator is only going to be according to your secret grant that you have been granted by the Creator, according to that dot that you can't see. It is not a material thing—can't be!

You must not balance *that* understanding with an ordinary balance—no. It is even beyond your mind, and beyond mind comes intellect. Your mind's connection is with the material aspects of this planet. You can balance this nature [that you observe] according to your mind's understanding; that means mind's level. But beyond that, above your mind, there is intellect. Mind may belong to our physical being, but intellect that *tahakkum*, controls, our physical being, that is its level. That belongs to our heavenly being.

That is the first step, that through your intellect you may find a way to understand your heavenly position. And when you reach that level, at that level, according to the level of your spiritual understanding, you may reach an understanding of the Lord of this planet—of *this* planet; you can't reach [an understanding of the Lord of] the universe. No; of this planet.

The biggest mistake of mankind now is that they are asking—sometimes believers are also falling into that mistake—to make the Creator according to their intellect, according to their spiritual level, to bring that One to *their* horizon of knowledge and understanding. Therefore, they are saying something that is never going to be accepted as Reality because your existence is not real existence.

The universe has never had a real existence. If real existence had been given to the universe, the universe would have been fixed, never moving, never changing, never disappearing. And now, when they look, they are saying "Black holes, black holes." Those black holes, gigantic galaxies are coming near to them and disappearing. If those gigantic galaxies have real existence, how would they disappear? No; can't be. They are only an appearance, a manifestation, of the existence of creation. He is the Creator, creating, and we are looking and saying, "Oh, we are in existence," and causing people to be mistaken about their Lord.

Don't use your intellect above your level of understanding; finished! You have been granted a level for understanding Allah. They are saying, "Beyond our understanding." You may reach endless horizons for understanding, but you should find *never-ending* horizons. Any limit you come to, His Existence, His Real Existence, is beyond that. And you are always going to be in the position of non-being. That means that we never have real existence, here or hereafter—no.

The Holy Name, *Samad*,[93] no one understands. *Samad* gives that meaning—now we are saying it—that [only] *He* is in real existence. All, everything—no space and no position for being in existence, only like an appearance [manifestation?], coming and going. Nothing of creatures has a real existence. *Hasha!*[94] That is *shirk!*[95]

---

[93]Eternal, everlasting.

[94]Never! God forbid!

[95]Attributing divinity or its attributes–in this case, reality and eternity—to created things.

Samad; you can't find any place, according our understanding, 'empty,' where He, His Existence, is not going to be there. No room for anything in His Existence. *Samad*—no room, no space, no place! You may say [that there are] millions, trillions like these universes, gigantic universes, but no room for them in real existence. They are not, they were never granted a real existence!

Lam yalid, lam yalid.[96] He never gives from His real Existence to anything, to anyone. Can't be! *M'arifat-Ullah;*[97] can't be! *Lam yalid;* He never gives from Himself *wilada.*[98] That means giving an existence to a baby, but Allah Almighty never gives from His real Existence to creatures— no! If we can find even less than an atom's space to put someone's existence into, that means that He does not control everything by Himself and someone may be in His Existence. No! Only He is in existence. "I am here. *Inni ana Llah,*[99] I am your Lord speaking to you , O Moses, no one else. Only I am that One, here."

Lam Yalid. He never granted real existence from His Existence to anything. *Qatt'an batil;*[100] never! Can't be, can't be! *Allah hua al-an kama kan. Allah hua Allah.*[101] He is Allah, who now, also, is only One. As He was in pre-eternity, so He is going to be in post-eternity, never anyone coming with

---

[96] *"He does not beget, [nor was He begotten]."* (112:3)

[97] Inner knowledge of Allah, gnosis.

[98] Begetting or bearing a child.

[99] *"Indeed, I am Allah"* (20:14), part of God's speech to Moses at the Burning Bush at Mount Sinai.

[100] Definitely false.

[101] Allah is now as he ever was. Allah is Allah.

Him—no. He never gives real existence to anyone. Can't be!

Therefore, we must use our intellect, and we have been ordered to use our intellect according to our understanding level, not to go beyond it—no.

I am looking here at trees that three months ago were only wood. Now they are *tazyin*,[102] decorated, with so many things, and we are thinking that it is a real existence. After six months, you will find that all of this has disappeared. Where are they now? Finished; no existence for them. If they had real existence, they couldn't disappear. The biggest mistake is to think about the Lord of the Heavens and to claim that we are also in existence. No! Each one of mankind that now is claiming "That one—I am that one," and never accepting to be no one but saying "Someone," after a while they are going to disappear, finishing.

So many events are written about in old books as tales, and tales may even be fairy tales. Doesn't matter! I heard and I read that India is the most diverse continent on earth, with so many, so many *'ajaib*,[103] surprising events, surprising plants, surprising animals. Such a rich continent you can't find as India. And its history is full of such surprising, astonishing tales. And so many kinds of people, so many tribes, they lived in it.

And our heedless Indian people are running away from such a rich continent and running to learn something in

---

[102]Adorned, ornamented.
[103]Strange, surprising, wondrous.

England, in Europe, even coming to Cyprus to learn something, and learning this only. All of them are heedless. They are not looking at what Allah Almighty granted to them. They are running away from India to find work, to live. They are such foolish mindless people, leaving India, coming to Europe. What is in Europe? Alcohol, adultery, foolishness, violence. Where are you coming? But, no-mind people. Allah granted them so many treasures!

There reached me a tale. In India, they were governed by kings and they were happy [chuckles] that there was no democracy for them. (These foolish ones are asking for democracy—Turks, Pakistanis, Hindustanis!)

Kings were governing, and due to their customs, when their king passed away, they were preparing his body and carrying him to his grave, not on shoulders or in a box like Christians or like Muslims. They put him on a *kızak*, sledge, with his head outside.

And the people were bringing it, saying "O-ooh! Our king is going. Oh-h!" They were dancing, very happy that that king who had been sitting on his throne, such a proud one, on his head his crown, in his hand his royal *'asa*, sceptre, and such clothes, at the end they were putting him on the sledge and his head did not reach the sledge, outside it. And they were bringing him, and his head was going "*Tak-tak, tak-tak, tak-tak*"; his head *vuriyor yeri*,[104] and they were bringing his head, also, on the ground. And the people were very happy. [Parodies:] "Yesterday you were a king, sitting on the throne. Today we are burying you. Because today you can't bring yourself, even, we are bringing you.

---

[104]Hitting the ground.

Look, O kings! Finally you should be like this." Use your goodness, use your best actions for your nation, or you are finally going to be like this."

And people they are not thinking about that no existence. It means that yesterday you had an existence to be a king, but today, no existence for you. We are carrying you to a field, graveyard, to put earth on you and to leave you under the earth, and to grow on it, on you, so much grass. Where is your existence, O people?

[Parodies:] "I am graduated from Pakistan," students. "We are graduated as Doctors of Physics, Doctors of Good Relationships" between Shaytan and people, *ogle mi*?[105] What is 'relationship'? Public relations. People are graduating, putting on their heads the hat of Western scholars and dressing like *garagar falklariya*, a black eagle, putting on a *jubba*,[106] also, and putting like this. "We graduated from the University of Europe, Europe University of Lefke—oh!" And then, it is not enough, also. "We are working to be Masters now, and after it to be Ph.Ds., also, doctors."

Where is your existence? Look at your kings in India, 2000 years ago. They were carrying him on a sledge to show people that there is no existence even for kings or emperors. "We are bringing him now to his graveyard and making his head to hit the earth, and we are bringing him to his grave."

---

[105][Tr.,] Right? Isn't it so?

[106]Academic robe.

O people, you are on the wrong way! All nations are going on the wrong way. Democracy is the wrong way, because democracy is making people to run away from their Lord, to run away from Reality. Democracy is cheating people, saying, "You have real existence," and there is no real existence except for the Creator. May Allah forgive us!

And Muslims, they are saying, "That is a big *'alim*,[107] big *wali*,"[108] and saying this one reached that [spiritual] station. There are no stations. There is only the station of servanthood, and our situation, our position, is only to be at the stage of servanthood and to say, "O our Lord, we are Your servants. No existence for us. Real existence is for You. All glory be to You, O our Lord! Forgive us and grant us, from Your endless blessings, to be happy with Your existence. We know we have no existence. Grant us existence only to look at Your unchanging, never-ending Beauty Oceans, to be there."

May Allah forgive us and give us some understanding. Therefore, everything is going to be at the level of our understanding, no more. No more; you can't carry it, you can't carry it! And we are speaking only at the lowest level of understanding, no more. And the levels of understanding are never-ending, *m'arifat-Ullah*. The knowledge about your Lord, the stages or stations of understanding, are never-ending; never-ending, also, from pre-eternity up to post-eternity.

O our Lord, grant Your mercy to Your heedless servants. Give us, from Your endless Mercy Oceans, some ones

---

[107]Islamic scholar.

[108]Saint, holy man.

to awaken us, to say, "O people, wake up and look at Reality." For the honor of the most honored one in Your Divine Presence, Sayyidina Muhammad ﷺ—*Fateha.* ▲

11

PROTOCOL FOR THE DIVINE PRESENCE

A'udhu bil-Lahi min ash-Shaytani-r-rajim. Bismillahi-r-Rahmani-r-Rahim. La haula wa la quwwata illa bil-Lahi-l-'Aliyyi-l-'Adhim.

It is an Association, *sohbet*. May Allah grant us what is necessary for our beings. But no one may understand that Allah Almighty is directing His servants directly; indirectly, *ghayri mubashir*.[109] We know or we must know that no one can be directly connected to their Lord's Divine Presence. Let alone mankind—even Sayyidina Archangel Gabriel ﷺ isn't able *mubasharatan*, directly, to reach the Divine Presence. Impossible! Impossible! Impossible!

But shu'un-Illah, the works of Allah or Allah Almighty's Actions, you can't balance them through your mind's balance. Impossible! He reaches directly to every creation, but no one among His creatures reaches directly to Him. He must be directly with every kind of creation without any mediator; otherwise it would be impossible for anything of creatures to be in existence because He, Almighty, is keeping every creature in existence by His divine existence. If He is not with His creatures directly, there can't be anything

---

[109]Without direct contact.

in existence. If you say that He is not reaching to His creation directly, that would mean that creature is in existence
by itself, by himself. Can't be!

You aren't able to reach to your Lord's Divine Presence
directly; no. You must be with a mediator, bringing you indirectly to His Divine Presence. His attribute is to reach
every creation Himself, and He must accompany everything, everything must be in His company.[110] His divine
dominion and hegemony must be with those creations, but
they are in need of a mediator. Allah is saying that He is
aqrabu ilayhi min habli-l-warid," [111] He is closer to you than
you yourself, than this too-life-giving vein. This vein is inside you, no distance, and He is saying, *"Wa nahnu akrabu
ilayhi min habli-l-warid, We are closer to him than his jugular
vein."* Although we are in need of a mediator to reach to
Him, He is "closer to us than our jugular vein."

Mutashabihat.[112] Qur'an al-Karim,[113] it is oceans. To understand it, it is not easy. If *Sahib uz-Zaman Mahdi*[114] ﷺ
comes, he will take away those meanings that are written
now around Holy Qur'an as a *ma'an,*[115] attempting to make a
commentary of the holy verses—taking all of them and
throwing them into the ocean or burning them. It is *haram*[116]

---

[110]*And He is with you [collectively] wherever you are."* (57:4)

[111]*"[And We are] closer to him [the human being] than his jugular vein."* (50:16)

[112]Qur'anic verses that are ambiguous or capable of different interpreta-
tions.

[113]The Noble Qur'an.

[114]The Man of the Time, Sayyidina Mahdi.

[115]Careful study, attentive scrutiny.

[116]Prohibited or forbidden, because such commentaries convey only the
basoc. obvious, external meanings, whereas the manifold and spiritual

to look at those translations [commentaries] of the Holy Qur'an. It is not your station, your place. You can't understand, because they are trying to put the ocean into a thimble. What is that—for what? They are trying to make people not to use mediators, saying, "You, by yourself [on your own], you can understand." What are you understanding? If I put a newspaper in front of you, you are not understanding!

The Holy Qur'an, for each letter, has at least 24,000 meanings. If you are saying "Alif, Lam, Mim,"[117] Alif must be granted at least 24,000 meanings and more, la muntaha laha[118]—no limit for the meanings of any of them. What is this, writing around the Holy Qur'an, printing and bringing to read? And so many people are coming and saying, "O shaykh, what you are saying we are not finding in it."

Muhiyuddin,[119] Allah bless him, he was saying that I will bring to you the names of all the prophets from the Holy Qur'an." There are 124,000 prophets [altogether]; what is mentioned in the Holy Qur'an is the names of twenty-eight prophets. And Muhiyuddin, Allah bless him, he was saying, "I can bring the names of 124,000 prophets."

And they were saying, "O shaykh, what are you saying? This is from where?"

---

meanings of each word, each letter, of the Qur'an are known only to the holy people of Islam, its saints (awliya).

[117]The Arabic letters corresponding to A, L and M, with which the second surah (chapter) of the Qur'an opens.

[118]No end, limit, ultimate boundary for it.

[119]Ibn al-'Arabi.

"Don't make me angry! (*awliya's* anger is a divine thing). I may bring all the names of Adam's descendants from the Holy Qur'an." *La hawla wa la quwwata illa bil-Llahi-l-'Aliyyi-l-'Adhim!"*

T'alim![120] Therefore, it is a teaching for nations that Allah Almighty used Archangel Gabriel ﷺ as a mediator to all the prophets, that people must know that it is not possible for everyone to reach to their Lord's Divine Presence directly, but they are in need to take a mediator.

We were in Athens last week. They brought a car and in it there was a tourist guide for showing us that city. And no one was saying, "Why are we in need of that person? Leave him! We can look everywhere."

You may look but you can't understand. You know nothing. If no guide there, you don't know this building, that building; this temple, that temple; that area, this area; that mountain, this mountain. What about for your Lord?

Therefore, the Holy Qur'an teaches those people who have been granted to be guides of the servants of the Lord of the Heavens.[121] No one is going to reach Allah directly—no; can't be. There is for everything a rule, or there is a protocol. For reaching the president or prime minister or minister or other high level people, there is a protocol among mankind. What about for you? You want there to be no proto-

---

[120]Training, instruction.

[121]That is, the Holy Qur'an teaches the teachers, the holy ones whom Allah has appointed as guides and teacher for the rest of mankind, who are empowered to understand its deepest meanings.

col for reaching to your Lord, and you are going erratically like this?

Then the protocol that we may be asking for to reach the *Sultan's* presence—perhaps a peasant is coming on his donkey and asking at the *madkhal*, gate, of the palace, coming, saying, "I am just coming to meet our king, yes. Let me come in!"

What would they say? "Come down off the donkey." And that ignorant peasant would say, "No, I can't because I am bringing something with me. I am coming from the *souq*, from the market, and on my way I wish to meet him. If I leave my donkey here, it may be stolen. Therefore I must be on my donkey to come into the palace and to meet him," talking like this.

Therefore, Abu Yazid, Sultan al-'Arifin was asking, "O my Lord, let me to come to You, to Your Divine Presence."

And the Lord of the Heavens was answering, *"D'a nafsik wa ta'al*—leave your donkey and come." But that peasant was asking to go on his donkey to meet the *sultan*, to meet the king.

That is the protocol, main protocol, never changed from *azal ila 'abad*[122]—never changed. *"D'a nafsik wa ta'al*—leave your mount and come in." You must get down and walking you must go.

Therefore, *mubasharatan*, directly, you can't reach to your Lord till you leave your ego, your mount that is your

---

[122]Pre-eternity to post-eternity,; that is, from the beginning to the end.

ego, and then coming in. And all *tariqats*[123] are asking to do this, to teach people and make them to practice.

Communist people and materialist people, they are saying that mankind, all of them, are on same level. No, not on the same level! Two levels, one riding on his mount; another, his donkey riding on him. Two kinds people in the entire world. *Wa la tansau-l-fadla baynakum*[124]—that meaning.

No; mankind, they are not on the same level. Some of them are riding on their egos. *Nafsuka matiyatuka*[125] — *nafs* is your horse or donkey or mount. Ride on it. Some of them are riding and some of them are carrying their horses on their shoulders. Two kinds of people; no third one, no third one. Anyone know a third one? No. Either riding or *piyade*, *mashat*;[126] riding on his horse or making his horse ride on him.

A horse is a noble creature but a donkey, its level is down, and our egos, their level is donkeys' level. People are two kinds: one rides his donkey and some people let their donkeys ride on them. Their level is under the level of a donkey. *Mubasharatun*; no, you can't enter the Divine Presence directly. You must keep the protocol, and the protocol is to leave your ego, leave your donkey, *barra*, outside, and come in. Those who leave their donkeys outside and come, the door is open to them. "Come!"

---

[123]Literally, "way." In this context, it refers to Sufi orders.

[124]*"And do not forget precedence [i.e., ranks] among yourselves."* (2:237)

[125]Your *nafs* [ego, lower self] is your mount.

[126]Walking.

"Come to My Divine Presence, O My servant. You are My servant. Others, they are servants their donkeys. They can't be here. Whoever is a servant to his donkey can't enter here; no. Those who have left their donkeys, they are My servants. Those who do not leave their donkeys, they are donkeys' servants, not *My* servants."

May Allah forgive me and bless you. For the honor the most honored one in His Divine Presence, who taught people the realities of being in existence and their importance and their missions, Sayyidina Muhammad ﷺ—*Fateha*. ▲

12

BEING SLAVES TO TECHNOLOGY AND DESIRES

We are most in need, in our time, to be humble because humbleness is the main attribute of servants. Humbleness is also the first attribute of prophets, and also humbleness is the first step towards becoming a holy man.

You must not be cheated by your knowledge or technology. As long as you have been given authority to take control on such powers, you must know it is only a favor. You must know that you may have all the authority of technology, but all technology can never give anything like a cup of water can give if you are thirsty; all technological improvements, if you are hungry, never give satisfaction.

Why is mankind coming in front of technology and bowing to it? *For what, why?* You must be humble, fearful, respectful, to that One who gives refreshment and satisfaction and life! Therefore, people are going on a wrong way in our day: they are making themselves like slaves before a powerful being, and they are not thinking about themselves and the origins of things. Who provides when hungry or thirsty? If that person is going to be in a desert and he needs a cup of water, he is ready to destroy all technology for a cup of water because he knows that cup gives life but all technology gives nothing.

Therefore, I am calling all Western people to be humble only to their Lord, not to technology. We must think about ourselves and we must try to make ourselves free ones for Allah's service only. Men are created as free ones, but after the age of maturity[127] they are becoming slaves.

You must try to save yourself from slavery, or you will live and die as a slave to Shaytan, to *dunya*, and to ego and to its desires, and we are trying to be free from every desire. Abu Yazid Bistami, he was saying, "I must not want. I am asking to want nothing."

Therefore, we are trying to leave every desire coming through our egos because desires are making people slaves. As long as you have more desires, you are caught and tied, but when you limit your desires, you are going to be free for the service of Allah. As long as you have more desires, those desires are making you their servants. Therefore, most people are slaves because they have hundreds and thousands of different desires, and it is impossible to fulfill all of them. And a holy man is a man free from every desire except to be a sincere servant to his Lord, Allah Almighty.

Therefore, I was with Grandshaykh for forty years and he was always asking to lessen desires so that we may not be slaves to our egos and desires. Every *tariqat* is trying to make its *murids* free from their desires. And I am asking forgiveness from Allah so that we may be ready for His divine service, and He will help us, according to our desires. If our desires are suitable for divine agreement, Allah will make you successful in reaching to His Divine Presence. ▲

---

[127]That is, after the time of puberty, they become slaves to sexual desires.

13

LORDSHIP IS FOR ONE

A'udhu bil-Lahi min ash-Shaytani-r-rajim. Bismillahi-r-Rahmani-r-Rahim. La haula wa la quwatta illa bil-Lahi-l-'Aliyyi-l-'Adhim. Allahu akbar wa lil-Lahi-l-hamd.

Two levels, the level that there is no other level above it (we are only saying this for understanding). That is the position of Lordship. And there is the position of servanthood.

Lordship is never going to be granted. It is not a grant to be given to any creature because no creature is able to carry that position. That position is only for One, and that One, He is the Creator. Impossible for someone else to be granted Lordship—no!

Christians, they are saying, "Our Lord, Jesus Christ." That is a big mistake—biggest mistake! No intellect can accept it, or never can our mind's capacity reach to an understanding of that position; never accepted. The biggest wrong is to say for Jesus Christ, "He is our Lord." No, he can't be, because Jesus Christ is a creature from among mankind. There is no 'god kind.' Can 'God kind' be? No, it can't be.

Countless mankind may come into imitation existence, but real Lordship, He, Almighty, is keeping only for Himself. No one is there to be suitable for carrying Lordship, because if there should be someone to carry Lordship, he must be in the same position as the first One. And if he is the same as the first One, that means you can't say "one, two." You should say, "Oh, this—this is the first one." If we are saying there is another one, what is his qualification? The same as the first one's!

Therefore, why we are saying "One, Two, Three"? It is only One, *One*. Without that One, there can't be another, a second one. He must put himself into the second one for him to be able to carry Lordship. That means only one.

Impossible, impossible! Same, same, and no room for another one just similar to the first one. Two without One can't be two; three without One can't be three; a hundred without One can't be a hundred, going to be ninety-nine.

Therefore, Lordship never accepts a *sharik*, partner. Allah, He is Lord. When you say, "Jesus Christ is Lord," what about the first One? Is He going to leave, to make Himself tired or to make Himself retired, or going to take Himself away from existence to give Jesus His Lordship? For what? Is Jesus Christ going to be His heir? Why? Is He tired or retired? But Christians, billions of them, never think about such things, to correct their beliefs, to glorify the Lord of the Heavens. They are saying this without thinking. And I am meeting so many of them.

They are reading their holy books but lacking proper understanding. Even though those books are different from one another, even then they are not understanding because they do not have enough light in their hearts. If you give a person a book to read it in darkness, what is he going to read or to understand? Therefore, there must be heavenly lights in that one's heart; when looking at holy books he may understand quickly. No one, up to today—I am meeting so many of them; even though reaching the top point among themselves, but yet they are not understanding.

Lordship is for only that One. What about others? That second level is for all creation, the divine stamp on them as servants. They are servants and their position is servanthood. No one can pass beyond that. But people—among Muslims, also—they like to make some persons above that level of common people. Maybe some people are going up, going up, but even though they may reach countless levels, their levels are still only the level of servanthood. Impossible, impossible! Glory be to Allah!

That thing is making troubles among people. No-mind people from *ahli dunya*[128] —common people who are not concerned about heavenly messages or heavenly ranks; they should be atheist people or communist people or materialist people or square-headed people or no-mind people, or descendants-of-apes people, who claim they are coming from apes[129]—they are also asking to make themselves in a distinguished position. Some of them through their beauty are thinking that our level is distinguished. Some of them through their mind-products, they are seeing themselves as different from others, saying, "Our level is not an ordinary level. The ordinary level is for common people."

---

[128]People attached to this world's life.

[129]That is, those who believe that higher life forms evolved from lower ones, and that human beings are nothing but a higher animal species rather than a unique creation of the Creator, endowed with conscience, intelligence, and granted the gift of eternal life.

Indian people, what are they saying? *Harijan, achut*, the lowest people in India, for whom they are saying, "No value for them. Animals and those are at the same level." But if going up, they are saying that we are distinguished ones. And when they are looking at themselves and saying "We are distinguished ones," they are asking to reach, at their distance, at their level, to look at themselves with another view and to say, "We are not like *those* people."

What is your opinion, when you are saying we are not like those people, unlearned people, laborers, farmers, peasants? "No. We are something good." No! I am asking what is your position? What is happening? When you are looking at yourself as higher, what is your difference?

They took me in Spain to a castle. Have you been there—a famous king's palace? So many priests were also there at that castle, palace on the mountains, of one king. And different kinds—Allah-Allah, Allah-Allah!—of religious people, priests and such people, they were showing me around.

Then they opened one room. There was a seat there, a wooden seat. Maybe that king was taller than Fulan, and that seat was twice as big as what I was sitting on there. I was saying, "What is that?"

"That it is the toilet place."

[In a shocked, low voice:] Toilet place? Toilet place? And he was thinking himself so high, such a high rank for himself, and *toilet, toilet . . .?* What happened? How? The toilet is carrying their real level. Whoever enters the toilet, what is their level? Understand?

Grandshaykh was saying that one person, his uncle, was sitting in a coffee shop, and one [young man came in and sat down]. Dagestan people, they are very proud people. That man sat down like this. And he was wearing a *khanjar*, dagger, the famous *khanjar* of Daghestan, and putting on his head this huge fur hat and making his hat like this. [pushing his turban at a cocky angle] [laughter]. .....Grandshaykh's uncle, he was over one hundred years, and saying, "O my son, do you not go to the toilet?" [Laughs.] And when he was hearing this, quickly correcting his head and straightening his hat.

And Allah Almighty is saying concerning Jesus Christ in the Holy Qur'an, "*Wahid, Wahid*"[130]—one word, making clear what we are saying. Everything that they are claiming for Jesus Christ, that he is Lord, and his mother is also given such a heavenly position, Allah Almighty is giving a description of them and saying, "*Kana yakulani-t-ta'am.*"[131]

O Christians who are saying that the level of Jesus Christ is Lordship, Allah is saying, "But they were, he and his mother, eating and drinking." Anyone eating and drinking must be in need of a toilet. What is that?

Therefore, I am saying concerning that king who was making himself above their level: as much as possible you

---

[130]"One, One," perhaps a reference to the verse, "*O people of the Scriptures, do not exaggerate in your religion nor say anything concerning Allah except the truth. The Messiah, Jesus son of Mary, was but a messenger of Allah and His word that He cast into Mary and a soul from Him. So believe in Allah and His messengers, and do not say 'Three.' Cease! [It is] better for you. Indeed, Allah is but one God* [ilahun wahid]." (4:171)

[131]"*They [Jesus and his mother] both used to eat [earthly] food.*" (5:75)

are making yourself high, but when your stomach begins to rumble, that says, "You can't be there, you must come down," and coming down to the dirtiest place, toilet, quickly running.

People are never using their intelligence, their minds, and ascribing to themselves something that is not for them. That is the source of *jahalat*, ignorance. That is the source of crisis, that is the source of wars and fighting, that is the source of saying, "Oh, we are Turks! No one can be like us." Arabs, they are saying, *"Nahnu-l-'Arab, ana-l-'Arab."*[132] They are thinking that being Arab gives honor to them. No! Never does Allah say *"Ya ayyuha-l-'Arab, ya ayyuha-l-ladhina 'Arab."*[133] *"Ya ayyuhal-l-ladhina amanu,"*[134] Allah is saying.

Where are the teachings of real Islam and the teachings of holy books? Are holy books asking from people to be servants, or to claim to be lords because they are putting something on their heads, or living in palaces or riding on famous horses or having treasures? All of them are not for you!

Two levels. And all prophets came to call people to their real position, to say, "We are Your servants." That is the real teaching of all holy books. No book has come and given more honor to mankind than servanthood. Can't be!

But servanthood is coming heavy on Satan and his followers, and he is saying, "No! You must claim that you are the most distinguished ones among creation and you are

---

[132]"We are Arabs, I am an Arab."

[133]"O you Arab, O you who are Arabs."

[134]*"O you who believe [in Islam],"* a phrase that prefaces a large number of Qur'anic commands and injunctions.

something, you are *something*." No, you are *not* something.
Your level is only servanthood.

That is summary of all the messages that have been sent
through messengers [prophets] to people. And what has
happened? 124,000 prophets came and gave the same message to people, and no one welcomed any prophet. No nation was accepting to say, "Welcome to you!" because
prophets came to put down their pride, to make them say,
"We are Your servants." But servanthood is so heavy,
heavy, for mankind.

That is what is happening now on earth. They are trying to be masters of this world—if not lords, at least to be
masters or patrons of this world. Still, that is nothing. Their
aim, real aim, is to be Lord. Can't be!

May Allah forgive us and grant you good understanding to think about it and to follow the ways of prophets,
who, all of them, are saying, "We are servants." If *they* are
saying, "We are servants," then what about for their followers? Should they say, "We are lords"? No!

But people they have left heavenly commands and they
are running after their egos. Egos are representing Shaytan
and Shaytan represents the first rebellious one in the Divine
Presence, who was claiming to be the Lord of all creation.
And he was saying "You—You are Lord above, I am Lord

on earth,"[135] as Nimrod was saying, "O Ibrahim, I am Lord on earth, you are Lord in the Heavens."[136]

And the same bad characteristic or worst characteristic, now it is with everyone. They are making young ones, also, to grow up with the same idea, to say, "I am a Nimrod. I am never going to happy for someone to be Lord to me. I live on earth and I am trying to be Lord on earth, not to be under the command of anyone that you are saying is in the Heavens."

May Allah forgive us and send us some ones with power to change their ways, to take away so many heads, rotten heads—to take them away and to bring new heads, understanding the level of servanthood, and trying to be servants and asking for the honor of servanthood. For the honor of the most honored one in His Divine Presence, Sayyidina Muhammad ﷺ—*Fateha*. ▲

---

[135]4:118-119, 7:16-17, 15:39-40, 38:82-83.

[136]Similar to 2:258, which reports the dialogue between Abraham and Nimrod.

14

ADAM'S HONORED CREATION

A'udhu bil-Lahi min ash-Shaytani-r-rajim. Bismillahi-r-Rahmani-r-Rahim. La haula wa la quwwata illa bil-Lahi-l-'Aliyyi-l-'Adhim.

Talibu-l-'ilmi faridatu 'ala kulli Muslim wa Muslimah.[137] May Allah grant us good understanding. But He does not grant His grant directly, *mubasharatan.* It is impossible, impossible! Instead, Allah Almighty teaches His servants through His chosen servants [prophets and saints]. They have a special structure through their physical being as well as their spiritual being. They are not same as common people. No, can't be.

He, Almighty, created Adam, He prepared him.[138] For no other creature is He going to make them or their designs directly Himself. That honor was only granted to Adam. *He* was giving his form, his design. Any other one you know about?

---

[137]"Seeking knowledge is an obligation on every male and female Muslim." *(Hadith)*

[138]That is, He made him from the materials of the earth with His own (non-material) divine Hands (38:75).

Angels? Angels, they are heavenly beings. Their creation is in another way, "*Kun fa yakun.*"[139] They are heavenly beings, and the Heavens are not material. Angels' existence is from divine lights. It is different from the existence of *ardiyun* things that belong to this earth, world. Our specialty, our creation, is one hundred per cent different from their creation.

Allah Almighty, He said in pre-eternity,[140] "O My angels, I am going to make a new creature."[141] He was addressing those who were present in His Divine Presence, heavenly being, angels. "I am making, *ja'al,* I want to make a new creation, and, according to My divine will and My divine desire, I want to dress him in the honor that no one [else] among creatures can reach. Can't be! I want to make a new creation and to dress him as my representative (more than deputy), giving him [and his descendants] that honor and making them to be My representatives and deputies on earth."

All the angels, they were saying, "We are ready for that honor, O our Lord."[142] *Subhanallah,* they were saying this, but they were not looking at that new one's creation. The Lord of the Heavens was saying this to the angels, and the

---

[139]The divine Word of command, [*"When He decrees* (or *intends) a matter, He but says to it] 'Be!' and it is"* (3:47, 16:40, 19:35, 36:82, 40:68).

[140]That is, at some distant past "time" in Allah's non-timed eternity.

[141]"*...Your Lord said to the angels, "Indeed, I will make a vice-gerent* [or *deputy] upon the earth."*(2:30)

[142]A paraphrase of the angels' response to Allah's proclamation concerning His new creation,"*Will You place upon it one who causes corruption therein and sheds blood, while we proclaim Your praise and sanctify You?"* (2:30)

angels they were thinking that that honor might be put on them, but it was impossible because they couldn't carry that.

Their honor is at another level, according to their creation, but that new one, he would be granted an honor that, till that time, no one had been dressed in. It had been prepared; the angels knew that, and they were looking and hoping it would be for them. But Allah Almighty was saying, "No; *that* one, who should be honored by being My representative and My deputy on earth." And that is the main *esas*,[143] foundation, on which the earth and everything on it is built. And He was saying, "No. I am creating that one. I am preparing that one. I am bringing that one. And he should be a new creature, to give something from Me to you."

Inna-Llaha khalaqa Adama 'ala suratih[144] — Allah Almighty created him. The Prophet is saying that whoever looked at him, it was like looking at their Lord, so great, so big an honor. All forms, all designs. belong to Allah; Allah Almighty, He has countless designs. He is that One that one of His Names is "Designer, *Musawwir*," and He likes to show from Himself according to the level of creation, not higher up—no. That is an impossibility; no possibility for Him [to do that]. But He granted to Adam a design that every creation may look and may understand something of His designs. And His designs are countless, unlimited.

Therefore, the Lord of the Heavens was saying [to the angels], "No, it is not for you. Your creation is different, and Adam's creation is going to be a very special one. I am mak-

---

[143]Fundamental, principal, essential, base, foundation.

[144]"Verily Allah created Adam in His likeness." Bukhari.

ing his form, I am the Designer for him. With My divine Hands, I am giving his form and his design."

Has any other creature that reached that rank? Therefore, even the worst person who is under the umbrella of mankind, he has also been granted that honor.

And Allah Almighty, by His Divine Hands, was giving Adam's form, and from Himself giving from His Divine Spirit, blowing into him. That is an honor that is impossible to be granted to any other one, from the beginning up to the end. Can't be! The last horizon or last limit or last level for all creation is to reach that point, but all of them are below the level of Adam and his descendants.

And when Allah Almighty directly created and blew into Adam from His Divine Spirit, he stood up and looked and glorified his Lord. Allah Almighty gave that honor directly to Adam first because he was the chosen one, the first chosen one.[145] Then Allah Almighty gave honor to Adam and his descendants, his children, indirectly—for common people, indirectly. Yes; doing this for all mankind.

When Adam was granted that, and he was standing up and glorifying his Lord, and was dressed in the real honor of being the representative and deputy of the Lord of the Heavens on earth, the angels were looking and saying, "This is another kind [of creature]. This is not from our level." And Allah Almighty ordered all heavenly beings, "Bow

---

[145]That is, Allah made Adam with His own divine hands and breathed into him something of His divine Spirit because he was the first of his kind, as well as being the first messenger to his kind. As for his progeny, they were created by the ordinary means of reproduction.

down, prostrate, to Adam," and they quickly made *sajdah*[146] because of that secret that Allah had granted to Adam of being His representative, *amru-l-'adhim*.[147]

That is an endless honor and glory. No other creature has been glorified by its Creator as Adam was glorified. The angels knew this and they quickly made *sajida*. Only Shaytan was getting angry, saying, "I do not accept Your command to prostrate to him!"[148] And he was saying, *"You created him from earth, but I am created from the flame of fire!"*[149] No *tamyiz*,[150] differentiation; he said this but he did not understand that Adam's creation was by Allah Almighty's Self, *bi-dhat*,[151] making his form by His own Lordship. He didn't grasp that point and he said, *"I am more honorable than him."*[152]

No. You were created by a [divine] order to be an angel or to be from the *jinn*, another kind of creation. Your creation is only by Allah's saying, *"Kun—be!"*[153] and you came into being, but Adam, He is the special Designer for Adam. But Shaytan never distinguished between this and that. It

---

[146]To bow down or prostrate. mentioned in the verse, *"And [mention] when We said to the angels, "Prostrate to Adam"; so they prostrated, except for Iblis.*

[147]The great or most important order.

[148]See 2:34, 7:11, 15:29-31, 17:16, 18:50, 20:116, 38:72-74.

[149]See 7:12, 15:33, 17:61, 38:76.

[150]Distinction, discernment, perception, judgment, realization.

[151]Self, essence, none other than.

[152]7:12, 38:76.

[153]The verse, *"Indeed, the likeness of Jesus with Allah is like that of Adam. He created him [Adam] from earth; then He said to him 'Be!' and he was"*(3:59), informs us that Adam's form was made by Allah from the materials of the earth and then given life by the divine word of command, *"Kun!"*

was so clear, but Shaytan was in deepest heedlessness, saying, "He is from earth, I am from the flames of fire."

He knows what you are saying. Why you are saying this? He is your Creator. Are you reminding or teaching Him that you were created from flames of fire and Adam from earth? You think that you aregoing to teach Him? *Hal min khaliqun ghayr Allah*?[154]—is there anyone else in existence as a Creator? Only Allah! Why are you saying this? But he was in deepest heedlessness.

Shaytan was created only by the holy command, "Be!" and becoming, from the flames, a new creation, *jinn*, and he was standing up and saying, "I am from the flames of fire and Adam is from earth."[155] But Adam was brought into existence in a special way, as his designer was his Lord Himself, Adam's Lord doing this. Arguing with Allah, saying, "I am from flame." What, flame? Flame, but Allah Almighty, *bi-dhat*, Himself worked on Adam. That is enough to reach that level of the limit of honor—enough! But Shaytan is never understanding, saying, "I am created from fire flame." Allah worked on you, for your creation, to make it? No, saying *"Kun! Be!"* and becoming Shaytan, becoming a *jinn*. But Adam was created another way.

The angels understood, falling down and prostrating to Adam, but Shaytan was saying, "No." Eh, go away. Never understanding! But now, step by step, through *awliya*, a new opening is coming, and they are targeting Shaytan and his goals, and beginning to *qadhaf*, to bombard the satanic

---

[154] *"Is there any creator other than Allah?"* (35:3)

[155] C.f. 38:76 *"(Iblis) said: 'I am better than he: thou createdst me from fire, and him thou createdst from clay.'"*

SHAYKH NAZIM ADIL AL-HAQQANI

mentality, beginning to cut that tree of pride in him. Little by little, little by little, this pride-tree is becoming—oh-h-h! Slowly, step by step, *awliya* are going at him to make him understand, giving him a *majal*, time, to think on it.

Now it is coming little by little, because the Day of Resurrection is approaching, that *awliyas'* bombarding him is beginning and making him know his position. Now he is still drugged because he is saying, "I am created from the flames of fire." [To Shaytan:] But Adam is not from fire. His Lord, by His own Hands, designed and formed him, bringing him into existence and saying, "You are My representative throughout creation, earth and heavens."[156]

Even though Adam was given his dwelling place on earth, his honor is for the Heavens, also. He may be here but he is not only the representative of Allah Almighty on earth but also in the Heavens. What we are saying, its proof is that the Seal of Prophets 鑼 , during the Night Journey,[157] saw Adam, and he was representing Allah Almighty throughout all creation. And because Adam was carrying the real representative of the Lord of the Heavens, Sayyidina Muhammad 鑼,[158] "If Muhammad 鑼 had not been brought into existence, no heavens or earth would be in ex-

---

[156]C.f. 2:30 *"Behold, thy Lord said to the angels: "I will create a vicegerent on earth."*

[157]The Holy Prophet's journey by night to Jerusalem, followed by his ascension to the Seven Heavens, where he was admitted to his Lord's Divine Presence.

[158]The meaning here is that, as mentioned in 7:172, because the seeds of all of Adam's descendants, including Muhammad 鑼鑼, were carried within Adam's body, Adam's existence was essential for Muhammad's physical existence but Muhammad's existence was essential for the existence of all creation: *Law lak; law lak, ma khalaqta'l-aflak.*

istence,"[159] *raghman*, in spite of Wahhabis and everyone who denies his holy honor. They are under the feet of that chosen one, under that most honored one's feet.

Therefore, we were speaking about Allah Almighty's making it obligatory for all believers to learn—*to learn what to learn*, to learn the truth of Reality and to learn about the true ones who are carrying that Divine *amanat*, trust. And this is a little bit of an opening, and after this are coming Oceans, Oceans, endless Oceans. And therefore we are saying that you can't learn anything without a teacher because mankind, they are in need of a mediator. Everyone must have a teacher because no one can learn something directly, but indirectly. Prophets are special beings and their inheritors [awliya] are special beings. You must try to reach one of them and to learn. If not, you should be *hattabu ahannum*, of no value. For those who are not learning, they should be in the dustbin.

May Allah forgive me, and grant to you to learn to understand. For the honor the most honored one in the Divine Presence, Sayyidina Muhammad—*Fateha*. ▲

---

[159]Hadith from Sayyiduna 'Abdullah ibn 'Abbas 🕮 related that: "Allah revealed to Prophet 'Isa 🕮 that: O 'Isa! Have faith (*iman*) in Muhammad and order your ummah to do the same. If Muhammad was not in existence, I would not have created Adam nor would I have made heaven or hell". Narrated by Hakim in his *Mustadrak* and Abu as-Shaykh in *Tabaqaat al-Isfahani'*.

15

STORY OF THE PIED-PIPER

A'udhu bil-Lahi min ash-Shaytani-r-rajim. Bismillahi-r-Rahmani-r-Rahim. La haula wa la quwwata illa bil-Lahi-l-'Aliyyi-l-'Adhim.

It is an Association. It is like a market, may be a mini-market, may be a mega- market, may be supermarket, may be another, hyper-market.

Eh, our market is a mini-market, poor people's market, so that they may be able to buy up to five dollars' worth or more, ten euu-ros, new money, eey-uros, oyruo. You can say such a foolish word? Eyuro, new name, new money. Eh, ten euros in his pocket, coming, asking to buy something that may be twenty euros. "Ten, write it down. I am paying ten." What shall we do? He is our customer. We must try to keep him.

Mini-market, but it has a special status. Yes. It is a group of people, a handful of people, but it is a different kind of group, because you may find in some places only one kind of people—from Turks or from Arabs or from French or from Greeks. *Harik;*[160] this is just different from other mini-markets because here you can find perhaps forty

---

[160]Unusual, extraordinary, marvelous, wondrous.

people but from thirty different counties, different nationalities, different languages, different cultures. Yes, it is small but it is like the *ayan kongre* of America, the Senate. Every kind of person may come here. That is a different status for our mini-market and that is its specialty. It is not from me, but it belongs to heavenly sources that everyone may be interested in, through heavenly springs, to drink from it or to wash himself.

Here are coming people who are asking for something. It is really difficult in our days to make a gathering [of people], to make people come without asking them to come, and you can't find people who would pay a lot of money to come and visit this place that is, amidst the largeness of this world, an unknown spot. Even Cyprus, the whole island, Republic, amidst the largeness of a huge map of this world, you can see only a very small dot; a very little, little space is given to it, and on the map, to find this place is so difficult. To look and to find and to ask to come here, it is an extraordinary happening now on earth. It is impossible to make people move from Moscow or from California or from Canada or from South Africa or from South America or from Europe, from England, from Germany, Japan, from China, from Malaysia, from Australia—to gather them. It is unseen or very rare. You may hear about it but you can't see it.

This is an introduction. We are making a way to Reality now.

What is the special position of this small place, and for there being here a handful of people? Why? Everyone coming here, they have different cultures. From Ceylon, also, people are coming, from Singapore coming, from Uzbekistan coming. Why? What is the reason?

I am giving food to them. [Parodies:] If someone comes from other groups of people to look, to enter into our kitchen, I am saying, "Give soup to this gentleman."

He is saying, "I am just, I, I . . .[making an excuse]."

"*Give soup!*"

"I can't," because he is looking inside [the soup].

But our people, they are never escaping; they are very happy. If there is a handful of flies in it, saying, "What is that?" and I am saying, "Mince."[161] First, Pakistani people, they are saying, "Very good, okay," and drinking [the soup]. "Where are they sleeping?" "Sleeping here. Best place, more than prisons" (prisons—may Allah keep you away from such punishment places!). You are free. You are sleeping here, eating, but you are free to go down, up and down.

Only I am angry with some ones in our groups. They are smoking. If I can catch that one, I will break his head because smoking and throwing away without thinking may cause a fire. Therefore, I don't like anyone smoking here. If I catch him, the next day I will say, "You must leave. Either you must leave smoking or leave our place."

This is a training center, to make them to leave bad manners, to leave *kufr*, to leave the ways of Shaytan, to kick out shaytanic teachings. That is the center's personality. We are trying not to let Shatyan come to this place, we are asking him to run away. And people, they are fed-up with

---

[161]Ground meat.

115

Shaytan and shaytanic traps and tricks, and they are asking to save themselves from those traps and tricks. They are going around [looking for a guide]; they are not coming firstly to me. They are asking for something, they are feeling [something] in their souls making them to ask for some safe place and clean place to save themselves, because Western countries, they are not clean countries; no.

Everything there is against humanity; everything is against our physical being, everything is against our spiritual being—all European countries, Western countries, including America, Russia, all countries. And our heedless Muslims, heedless Muslim countries, are asking to be like them.

I am sorry to say this, because our nation is asking to follow them, to be a member of that group of people who are making advertising, daily advertising, for the tricks and traps of Shaytan, to make people fall into them, for their egotistical desires, also.

Therefore, this is a center against Shaytan, against everything that is harming humanity, hurting humanity, destroying humanity, destroying the rights of human nature. Shaytan is playing with them—playing with them, cheating them, and they are asking to cheat people.

With which things? With everything that may give a kind of pleasure to people; but they are not really tasting that pleasure because a person may understand, when his mind is working, whether a thing gives them pleasure or not. When they are drinking they are losing their minds; they are losing their minds. They never understand if they have reached the pleasure that they are asking for, because a drunk person, how does he understand?

Someone was asking a person, "Sleep, what is its taste?" and he answered, "I have never tasted the pleasure or taste of sleep because when I sleep I know nothing. When I awaken, sleep has left me. Therefore, I never know if sleep gives me pleasure or not." A drunk person, when he is drinking, his mind has just stopped; out of order, the minds of drunk people. How they are going to *tamyiz*, distinguish, if it is pleasure or not? No.

Therefore, everything that they are making a big advertising for everywhere in Western countries, it is the biggest foolishness and biggest blame on mankind to run after those people. When they are drinking, they are tasting nothing; no—finished. Therefore, Shaytan and shaytanic methods are making the biggest trouble for heedless mankind. And mankind, they have lost their humanity, and humanity is an honor for them but they are leaving that humanity, falling to the level of animals. *That* level is mankind's level [now].

When you reach up from the level of animals' world, you should find humanity. Humanity, it symbolizes the perfection of mankind. If a person is going to be drunk and do every evil, every dirty thing, do you think that that gives honor to mankind? Whoever is preventing himself from falling down to the level of animals, that one is given honor and dressed in the honor of being from human nature; but under it, they are on the level of animals, either to be like herds or to be like violent, wild animals.

We are fighting this. We are a small group, but our aim is to prevent mankind from being at animals' level. We are trying to make them to be fixed and to reach to humanity, which is the honor among creation. Not any animal, not any other creature, has reached that honor. That is our goal.

We know that everything that belongs to *dunya* and its treasures is not for you, it is not for me. No one has been able to keep something from *dunya* forever for himself. And people, they are not taking their lessons from the pharaohs, how they carried *dunya*, the treasures of *dunya*, under those pyramids—what they reached. And they have been kept protected by making them mummies. Now, if you are looking to their faces, you can't eat for forty days; you can't sleep, also, from such an ugly and *y'arra*, disgusting, thing, running away.

I don't think that anyone goes into the pyramids. But if you bring that mummy to an ordinary place, I don't think that anyone, if you gave one billion dollars to him to sleep with him in that room up to morning, he would ever accept. Why? Their physical being has come to be in such an ugly form and its smell is so bad a smell; they are saying, "We don't like it." Perhaps they may say, "We will die by morning from being next to Pharaoh, and we are going to leave that one billion dollars, also."

O people, you must think about it. Enough, your following shaytanic ways, . enough falling into the tricks and traps of Shaytan. Now there is coming windy weather, what you call a typhoon, carrying away everything of those people, never remaining on earth such foolish people who are insisting on following the ways of Shaytan. Now the time is over!

Therefore, these people are coming from different countries to be ambassadors from here to their people, to their friends, to their families, to their nations, if they are clever ones. If not, perhaps if they can save themselves, it is okay.

May Allah forgive us. That is the reason that the pure nature of people is carrying them to such humble but powerful meetings, while it is very rare to find such meetings in the world throughout East and West. May Allah forgive us and send us a powerful shepherd, endowed with heavenly powers to carry people to where he is going.

There is a tale about a flute player (German people, they know better than me). Once upon a time there were many, many rats in a town in Germany. Yes; Hamelin. They were terrible creatures. Each one, if a hungry person made it into shawarma and ate, it would be enough, so *besli*, fat. Running everywhere; when people sat at the table to eat, they were jumping on the table, jumping on the heads or shoulders of people, and if a person took something to eat, another rat would steal it and bite him and eat it. They were biting cats, also, cats fearing them.

And then one day, a stranger with a flute came, passing through that town. They were looking.

"Who are you?"

"I am a stranger, going around."

"How do you live?"

"I play my flute, I live by playing my flute."

"What is the benefit of your flute?"

He said, "I have so many kinds of *hawa*, melodies. If I play, animals may run after me."

"Oh, very good! Look, we are sitting down now to eat and you will see what is happening to us."

They were making him sit and putting food to eat. So many rats rushed on it, some of them biting his ear, some biting his hand. He wasn't able to eat. He said, "It is for me to save you from these rats."

"Okay! If you do this, we will pay you a lot of money, to be happy. Yes."

"How much will you give to me? I am asking." (There was no Euro at that time; perhaps marks, or instead of marks, there were the golden coins of the empire). And they made a contract that they should give him a hundred coins. Okay.

And he went out, beginning to play the flute. All the rats came after that person. He was walking and playing, and they were running. And he went into the river, and all of them came, falling in it, and the water took them away. And then he was coming back and saying, "Pay me. What I was asking, give it to me."

Reis baladiya, mukhtar, mayor, the mayor of the city, he was saying, "What did you do?"

"One hundred."

"One hundred coins! What is that? Your flute-playing is never going to be worth more than one coin."

"Look, I made a contract. I would like my payment here, now. If not, I know what I am going to do to you."

Subhanallah! They were insisting not to give it and he said, "Leave that one coin also for yourself. I am going."

And he began another melody, and all the children, young ones, began to run after him, running, running, running. And the people, they were *nadam*, regretful, calling, "Come and take your pay!"

No. He was playing and small ones were running after him, coming to a hill like a bell. Going there, and an opening appeared, and that strange person entered and all of them went into it, disappearing.

This is a story [showing how] Allah Almighty is asking to gather His servants. He can do everything, but those who are [not responding,] they must, they should be punished. For the others, [Allah will] send someone whom they may follow to save themselves. We are looking for that one to do this.

For the honor most of the honored one in the Divine Presence, Sayyidina Muhammad ﷺ, Mahdi ؏, and then Jesus Christ, 'Isa ؏ —*Fateha*. ▲

16

MANKIND HAS BEEN GRANTED WILLPOWER

A'udhu bil-Lahi min ash-Shaytani-r-rajim. Bismillahi-r-Rahmani-r-Rahim. La haula wa la quwwata illa bil-Lahi-l-'Aliyyi-l-'Adhim.

We must believe. We must believe that only One's will is going on, only One's will is acting. No one else's will may force anything to be done. Only His will must be, for everyone's desires must be related [coordinated] to His Divine will.

Yes, our Lord, Almighty Allah, just granted to us, as an honor, will power, but we have been ordered also to know, to accept, that only His will is in effect. Because. He created man to be His representatives, to be His deputies, to be His caliphs on earth, He granted them will power. That is an honor that was never granted to any other creatures—no.

Even angels, they haven't been granted will power. They are directly under His will. The animals' world, animals' level, which is under the level of mankind, they also they haven't been given will power; no. All of them are moving, working or acting by His Divine will. But mankind has been granted it.

When a person is granted an honor, he must be given a responsibility. Otherwise he is going to be a ordinary worker, an employee with no responsibility. The responsibility belongs to his master whose command he is under; he does not use his own will as long as his master keeps that honor with himself. Then, when going up and given an honor, he must be loaded, also, with responsibility. Therefore, mankind has been granted that honor, and at the same time they have been asked by the Lord of the Heavens to do everything under His will. That means that you can use your will, but you can't ask for your will to be over His will.

The one who is asking for something to be according to his will, he is going to fail. For what reason? For his bad manners. He has bad manners because he is asking to have his will go on and never observing or being concerned with his Lord's will. He may say, "I wish this, I wish that. I like this, I don't like that."

Everyone is doing this, and we are passing through hundreds of events daily. For every action that we are intending to do, we are insisting, saying, "I like it to be . . ." — for example, "I like that one to be for me." Or he may say, "I like this thing to be as I like," never leaving a chance for his Lord's will, saying, "I like it, I don't like it."

Who are you? You are the master or you are a worker? You are the *sultan* or you are a servant? People have just forgotten now in our days that they are servants. They are trying to break down servanthood, and everyone is asking to be [a master]. "I am here. I am *sultan*. I am king. I am ordering. I like this. I don't like that." That is the biggest mistake of servants, to try to break down the *Sultan's* will.

Now the whole world is running after that way. Everyone is saying, "I want to be a commander. I want to be a judge. I want to be an M.P. I want to be a big businessman.

I want to be President. I want to be Number One. That is my hobby, that is my lifestyle. I like that style of life that everywhere I must be Number One and everywhere I want everything to be as I like. I never accept any other one's will—no. I am thinking only about myself. I want to be everything as I like!"

That is the worst characteristic of our ego. That means that he wants to break down his servanthood and to claim to be the Lord of people, as Pharaoh was saying to people, "You are all my servants and I am your Lord,"[162] or as Nimrod was saying to Abraham 丞 , "Oh, I am the king of the lands, king of the whole world, and your Lord is in the skies. I don't want Him to be involved in my work. I am free to do everything as I like.

"I do not understand, O Abraham! You are coming, saying something about the Lord of the Heavens. I don't care about this because I am Lord on earth and your Lord is in the skies, in the Heavens." And now, the same characteristic is covering the whole world, and people are going to be every size of Nimrod—small size, medium size and king size. Army people are saying, "We have power." Second, civil governments are saying, "Power is with us and we are going to do everything as we like." And youth, youth—because governments are urging them and saying, "You must learn. You must learn because the more you learn, the more you will reach the top level of servanthood and you may step into the area of lordship. When you reach the top point of your education or studying, then you may look at yourself and you may say, 'I like that one, I don't like this one!'"

---

[162]79:24.

Throughout the whole education of people and their studies, they are saying, "Oh, when I am finishing, I must go to London. It is not enough to be in Malaysia or Brunei or Singapore or Thailand or China or Pakistan. Their universities, they are not well-known, and I want to be someone well-known. If anyone asks me, 'Do you have any degree?' I can say, 'Yes, I have a degree from Oxford.' That one will say, 'And also you, my friend, you have such a degree?' 'Yes, sir. I am graduated from Cambridge.'"

Yes. Everyone wants to show himself, that we reached a point where we left off being ordinary ones on earth. We are claiming to be top level people. We don't like to be on servants' level. We like to be on the Lord's level. True, or not?

We are now going to complete our Association. Everyone wants to reach a level that can never belong to servants, asking to be on the level of Lordship—to order, not to be ordered; to order, to be commander, and others his servants.

We were saying that people say, "I like this, I like that." Allah granted His servants from His Divine attribute [of will] to want something according to their wills, but they must put their wills under His Will, and they may say, "If my Lord wants this, I like it. If my Lord does not want, if my Lord is not happy with my will, I am taking my will back and I am looking at His will."

We were speaking on that "Ya man kulla 'asirin 'alaika yasir,[163] O that One!" We are speaking on the illnesses, we

---

[163]"O He for whom every difficulty is easy!"

are speaking on the bad characteristics of egos. We have been authorized to speak on it, as well as for *tedavi*, to make a cure for it. That word that was coming to me, when I was sitting here, was to say to Allah, because that [making things easy] is His Divine Attribute, "O my Lord, O that One! Every difficulty that we are going to face, all kind of difficulties, they are difficult for us, but the only One who makes difficulties to disappear, to go away, to finish, to be easy, it is only You. You can do that. All the difficulties that Your servants from among mankind are going to face, they must not run there, here, leaving You and asking for an easy way, some ways to reach their freedom to save themselves from difficulties. Only by Your Will is it going to be, not by our wills."

If all people's wills came all together, it would still be impossible to make the difficulties that are among them to be solved or to reach an easy way. That is very important. Don't think that you, by yourself, can save yourself from difficulties; no. If your wills, all mankind's wills, came together, they couldn't find a way to get out of this closed area, because you are inside it. It is just closed on you, and the key—the One who put you in that closed area, the One who imprisoned you, only He can give you a way to get out, like the Children of Israel, Allah Almighty giving His judgment, Divine Judgment [after they disobeyed Moses ﷺ].

"For forty years, I am imprisoning you in *Tih sahara*, the area of Mount Sinai—for forty years, finished! You are inside. I am enclosing you. I am keeping the key. I can open it but I am not going to open to you because I am giving My just judgment that you should be punished for forty years in that prison."[164] And it was a free land—a free land but they couldn't escape. All of them passed away and were buried in that area.

Now all mankind, it is just closed on them, the key in my pocket. I am the weakest servant to be 'porter' for them. I closed it, keeping the key with me. All of them are inside. Till they are coming, asking freedom from Allah Almighty, then He may order me to open and I may open the door, otherwise the whole world may die, all of them. Without that key, they can't get out.

May Allah forgive us and bless you, for the honor of the most honored one in His Divine Presence.

I am nothing, but Their order is passing through [me], like that şeride, electric wire. If giving power, you can't touch it; if not, it is an ordinary wire. I am nothing; when I say this, I am saying the truth. But when they are ordered to be free, the Lord of the Heavens giving permission, when they are coming and saying, "O our Lord, save us. Save our selves, save our souls, S.O.S., S.O.S., S.O.S, S.O.S., O our Lord," then opening. If they are not asking this, let them come under oceans, finishing.

---

[164]C.f. Numbers 14:33-35 "Your children will be shepherds here for forty years, suffering for your unfaithfulness, until the last of your bodies lies in the desert. For forty years—one year for each of the forty days you explored the land—you will suffer for your sins and know what it is like to have me against you.' I, the Lord, have spoken, and I will surely do these things to this whole wicked community, which has banded together against me. They will meet their end in this desert; here they will die."

Also C.f. Qur'an: 5:26 "(Their Lord) said: For this the land will surely be forbidden them for forty years that they will. wander in the earth, bewildered. So grieve not over the wrongdoing folk."

May Allah forgive us. For the honor of that most honored one, *bi-hurmati-l- Fateha.*[165] ▲

---

[165]For the honor of *[surat-]* al-Fateha.

17

800 FORBIDDEN ACTIONS

A'udhu bil-Lahi min ash-Shaytani-r-rajim. Bismillahi-r-Rahmani-r-Rahim. La haula wa la quwwata illa bil-Lahi-l-'Aliyyi-l-'Adhim.

When Adam ﷺ landed on earth and his descendants spread around this world, some of them obeyed their father's commands, trying to keep those heavenly commands on earth.[166] But some of them refused to obey.

One group obeyed the holy commands that Adam ﷺ had brought to his descendants and some others made themselves free. And they were saying, "We are not following your commands. We do not believe what you are saying and our feelings are directing us to be free ones. We are asking for freedom. We never like to be under any command—no. We like to be free ones." Therefore, people split into two different parties, one of them asking to keep the holy commands and the second party asking to be free from any command that had been sent from the Heavens to the first prophet, Sayyidina Adam ﷺ.

---

[166]See 2:38.

When Satan was thrown out and kicked down to earth, he swore and said, "O Lord of the Heavens, curses have come on me due to Adam,[167] and I am going to take my revenge on his descendants. I am going to run after them to prevent them from following Your commands, Your heavenly orders. I shall try as much as possible, as much as possible, to make them not listen to Your holy commands. That curse on me must come on them, also!"

And when he was thrown out of the Heavens and landed on earth, from that day up to today he has never rested, he has never slept, he has never become tired; saying, "I must follow each one of Adam's children, not to be obedient ones, to be cursed ones. You are giving to them the honor of being Your representatives on earth, but I am going to run after them not to accept to be Your representatives. I shall make them follow me, to be *my* representatives!"

Then the divine command addressed the cursed one: "Do anything, if you can. Go, demon, and try to do what you are asking to do with them. Whoever follows you, whoever is with you, I will catch all of you finally and I will put you into the Fire."

And finally Shaytan began his work. How was he going to do this? He was so *shaytani*, evil, with such dangerous ideas for making the servants of Allah not to obey Him, Almighty. How did he succeed?

He was saying, "O children of Adam, look at those people who are obeying Adam. They are not free ones.

---

[167]The Qur'anic references for this and the following two paragraphs are 4:118-119; 7:16-18; 15:35, 39-44; 17:62-65; 38:78, 82-85.

They can't do as they like. I am calling you to be with me. I am taking away every order that is making you to be servants, I am making a free life for you on earth—a free life. Freedom to you! Come with me and live as you like. I am putting my flag, on which is written 'Freedom!'

"Let Adam and his obedient children keep orders, which are a heavy burden on them. They can't live as they like. Leave them suffer, to put themselves always under control, and they are restraining their desires because there is a heavenly order making some desires okay, *halal*, granted to you, and some forbidden. Whoever comes with me, I am not ordering you anything—no. I am opening for you a land where everyone may live as he likes. No any obligation on you, nothing forbidden for you. Nothing is forbidden for those who follow me."

And from that time up to today, these two parties, their struggling is continuing, their fighting is going on, and satanic freedom is attracting people. And people are running after Shaytan because his attraction that promises people unlimited freedom is gathering people to run after him. From that time until now, step by step, step by step, people are running and asking for freedom, unlimited freedom. And now we are really near the last day of the life of this planet; we are approaching it. And you are looking and seeing everywhere that satanic freedom just reached to the top point, top point of freedom.

Allah Almighty made a ban of eight hundred activities or doings or thinking in such a way. It is a tablet, and eight hundred kinds of satanic freedoms are written on it. The Seal of Prophets ﷺ brought it, and it lists eight hundred things that Satan is calling people to do, to follow those freedoms. It is just eight hundred; can't be 801. The limit of mankind for doing those accursed and worst actions or activities reaches eight hundred; no more power to go further after that point, to ask for more freedom. And we have, in our days, just reached that Prophet's tablet on which are written eight hundred forbidden actions and activities.

One, two, three, four, five—every forbidden thing people now are doing. It is now for them the last point of freedom, under the flag of democracy. The democratic system gives people unlimited freedom to do everything as they like; nothing is forbidden, and the top people have unlimited freedom. They give more courage to people [to do as they please].

First, they are making men waste their precious lives with something that has no meaning, no *fayda*, benefit. Shaytan is making millions of people [occupied with] football. What football—one ball? Yah. Billions of people, not millions—billions of people are running after this, wasting their lives for this. What is that, what is that foolishness?

And, *subhanallah*, I was always angry with that because, from childhood up to thirty years, people they are drunk with football. I was so unhappy [about that], and I was throwing out that bad desire that people are just running after. Then, from our [spiritual] Headquarters, a message was sent to me, saying, "It is as you are saying, showing that people are just occupied, billions of them, with that football. O shaykh of this time, you [already] know, but we are saying to you (perhaps someone may ask):

"It is a very good, very good idea of whomever has brought that football. Throughout the whole world they are playing and occupying the heads of people, whose heads are only like a football; nothing in them, empty heads. You must be thankful because they are occupied with that football. If that football had not come into being, those people, billions of people, would run after worse activities such that you couldn't find any way to save people.

"Leave them! Millions, even though they are thinking only about it and watching it for some hours daily or the whole day or weekly throughout their lives, they are prevented from worse activities. Leave them, but say to them that that is a satanic activity that to makes people not to pray."

They are occupied with football, and football is preventing them from thinking about anything else. and they are forgetting their servanthood in the Divine Presence, and they are wasting their lives. But after this, then there are 799 other prohibited things that are harming humanity through their honor and destroying mankind physically, destroying humanity spiritually, under the umbrella of democracy.

People are running to have full freedom, where everyone must speak; everyone must be free; everyone is asking to live as he likes. But this is also a dream that is never going to be reality; no. They are taking up the flag of freedom and using it only for cheating people, and for some [corrupt] ones, making common people reach their habits, to reach their aims. And men commonly, they are never given anything that they are asking for, never granted absolute freedom—no. The headquarters of that system of the world, governing systems, they are only cheating people. They are first class liars, first class cheats, first class wild people, first class violent people; no mercy with them, no justice with them, no good quality with them. They are just representatives of Shaytan—head ones, not feet ones. Feet ones, also, feet ones always kick—kick and cheat and kick.

Only for a few people, that [absolute] freedom. They want to do everything as they like—to use nations, to use men and women, for fulfilling their bad, their worst desires, so that all nations, all mankind, are either going to be representatives of Allah or are going to be cheated by devils, and they think that they are representatives of shaytanic life, and running and running, and never reaching anything.

O people, we are making you to take care. It is a warning. People they are every day crying and they are saying, "Oh, so many people killed here, so many people killed there." We are seeing that they are *asif*, they are so sorry about those events, but they are never asking what is the real reason. And they know nothing to stop it.

If a physician understands what is the problem with his patient, he may cure that one. If not understanding, no cure. Now, in all the world they are—I am not saying *like* drunk, they *are* drunk ones. They don't know how they will cure terrorism, how they can stop that violence on earth. I am saying, "Look in the East and West, what you are finding. Your armies, your nuclear bombs, your tanks, your guns will never finish that. It is growing."

There is a kind of grass that, if you cut it, after a while it comes up because its roots were not taken away. Roots, that is enough. After a while you are looking—"Oh-h! We were thinking that we had finished it. Now, growing again." If you do not reach the real reason, it is impossible to finish by guns, by planes, by rockets.

By having guns, you can't do anything. You must leave Shaytan, you must leave Shaytan! You must understand into which trap you are falling, with which trick people are coming into the trap. You must know this. If you do not know this, *impossible!* All nations should die, but violence is never going to be finished till people understand that that is a shaytanic way, making people kill each other.

Allah Almighty never ordered to people to kill each other, but Shaytan is saying, "Kill! Kill and don't be sorry. Kill them! Don't be sorry! Billions of people, half of them may die, and then whoever remains can take their rest." No! They are like those harvested fields [of grass], after a while going to stand up as it was. Till people leave Shaytan, terror, terrorism are never going to be ended.

That is only what we can say. Those who can understand may save themselves. If not, leave them. Don't be sorry, don't be sorry. *"Wa la tahzan 'alayhim.*[168] O My beloved one, don't be sorry about those people whom you are calling to Paradise but they are running to Hells and burning. Don't be sorry. You are calling them to Paradise, but they are rejecting you and running to the Fire. Leave them, burning."

Allah granted to His servants a mind to use it and to obey, and through their minds' power to choose a peaceful life with heavenly commands, keeping heavenly orders and being happy here and hereafter. Those who are refusing, they should be punished here and hereafter.

May Allah forgive me and bless you. This is only what we must understand. Now we have no power in our hands.

---

[168] *"And do not grieve over them* [the deniers of faith]." (15:88)

Power is with Shaytan and his representatives. You can't do anything. Leave them. You are not *mas'ul,* you are not responsible, for those who are running to the Fire. The Fire should burn them. *"Wa la tahzan 'alayhim wa la takun fi day-qin mimma yamkurun.*[169] O My beloved one, don't be sorry about them, and don't be in unrest in your heart because they are making so many tricks and traps for you and for your Message. Don't worry. *I* am looking after them. They should find their punishment through each other. Leave them."

Therefore, what can we do? We are waiting only that heavenly support comes for Allah Almighty's good servants. Even though they may be only a handful of people, but as the Prophet ﷺ was saying, "If, from my nation, twelve thousand are of the same heart, on the same way, no power can take them away. They should be victorious."[170] We are looking for those ones.

May Allah Almighty make it come quickly and save Islam and Muslims from the hands of devils, the representatives of Shaytan, as soon as possible. May Allah grant us His divine support from the Heavens for weak and poor Muslims. For the honor of that most honored one in His Divine Presence, Sayyidina Muhammad ﷺ—*Fateha.* ▲

---

[169] *"And do not grieve over them or be in distress concerning what they conspire."* (27:70)

[170] Referring to the Prophet's words, "...twelve thousand will not be overcome through smallness of numbers" (Abu Dawud, 2605).

18

Sight of Them Reminds of Allah

A'udhu bil-Lahi min ash-Shaytani-r-rajim. Bismillahi-r-Rahmani-r-Rahim. La haula wa la quwwata illa bil-Lahi-l-'Aliyi-l-'Adhim.

Nothing can be more precious than *'ilm*, knowledge. Knowledge gives honor to mankind. And *"Rutbatu-l-'ilmi 'ala-r-rutab,"*[171] *Rasul-Allah*, the Seal of the Prophets, the most honored one in His Divine Presence, Sayyidina Muhammad, Allah bless him and give him more glory, was saying.

There may be so many *rutbat*, ranks, for mankiind. Ranks all belong to this life, and most ranks they are artificial, they are not real ranks. That rank that is artificial just reaches up to the death of that person. When that person dies, his ranks also disappear because they are artificial, not real. Real ranks are heavenly ranks, which are grants from the Divine Presence to His servants.

Those ranks can't be granted to everyone—no. Heavenly ranks are only for certain people who are chosen ones among all mankind. How are they chosen? Who chooses them? Who are they?

---

[171]"The rank of knowledge is above [all] ranks." *(Hadith)*

It is not like an election of people, people voting and bringing the worst one on top. They are not elected or chosen by mankind; it is not from people—no. They are chosen and elected in the Heavens.

Who are they? They are those who, *idha ruhu, dhukir Allah*.[172] There are some people that, if you look at them, immediately you remember Allah and you say "Allah!" That is their specialty. They are just different ones from other people; their dressing is different from others.

"What is their dressing, O shaykh? Are they following fashions, dressing every time in a new fashion, following fashions? What is their dressing?"

Shaytan is playing with people through fashions, making people to rush and to run to keep fashions. Now the whole world is running after a new fashion for everything. They may say, "Our furniture is now old-fashioned. Now a new year is coming. We must change it for new-fashioned furniture." If he has a car in December and January comes, he says, "No, my car is now old-fashioned. I must look for a new fashion. New year, new fashion!"

For everything, men have so bad a habit now. Bad habits are just planted among mankind. Everyone is asking for a new fashion, new things. They are thinking that if they use new-fashioned clothes they are going to be changed to another personality; they are thinking that their physical being is going to be changed for the reason of new-fashioned clothes. Therefore, they are throwing away [so

---

[172]"[He who], when you see him, you remember Allah." *(Hadith)*

many clothes]. Everyone's wardrobe is full of clothes. If you are asking, "Why are you not wearing this that you were wearing last year?" [he may say,] "Now we are asking for new-fashioned clothes."

They are such square-headed people, no-mind people, who are thinking about new-fashioned clothes! It is the same clothes, same material, only sometimes [there is a slight difference]. Jackets—I was seeing that sometimes they have only one button. Then after a while, I am seeing that, oh, they are using two buttons. Now I am seeing if it is going to be one, two or three. They are not wearing one button [now]; it is so blameable for them. "No, it can't be. How can it be? *Moda*, fashion, new fashion, is three buttons. How you are coming with this?"

Sometimes you are seeing that those jackets are of one style and color, and trousers another. Sometime the trousers' bottom, this, is so large, and then [later] I am looking and it is like this. A [chimney] pipe? [Laughter.] Yes. "Because we are civilized people and we must follow fashions. Heh-heh-heh!"

What is the benefit? Shaytan is making them *maskara*;[173] Shaytan is playing with their small minds. The people now on earth, they are occupied by such foolish habits. A hundred per cent foolish habits they are, particularly for women. Women are running after fashion, new fashion followers.

[Parodies:] "We must look at this TV, how she is dressing. We must dress like that one."

---

[173]Ridiculous, butt, laughing-stock.

"O my darr-ling, you must also dress like this one."
[Laughter.]

And people, they are thinking that their clothes give
them honor, and then finally, when they die, everything is
taken from that one, all new fashions, nothing on her or on
him. You can't look at their faces.

Shaytanic teachings. And then Shaytan is using his representatives from devils, who are the new fashion makers.
Satan's representatives for new fashions, their headquarters,
where it is? In Paris—Paris, the new fashion center. People
are looking; new fashions are coming from Paris. English
people are not too much running after such things. They are
conservative people; they are keeping their old systems
much more, particularly Scottish people are never changing—yes? Scottish people, they are wearing what their
grandmothers, grandfathers, wore when they were using it
for a wedding ceremony.

And Germans [much laughter], they are also using
leather trousers from their ancestors. I don't know to where
their ancestors were reaching; from the time of. Emperor
Charlemagne or Wilhelm, using this and keeping it very
[carefully]. "We must keep this."

Subhan-Allahi-l-'Aliyyi-l-'Adhim! Shaytanic teachings,
and also Shaytan's representatives, are training people everywhere. Yes. "You must follow this because your honor,
top honor, is to follow fashions perfectly." [Parodies:] "This
year's fashion is yellow clothes, yellow hats, yellow *kravat*,
tie." Only priests, are not following that fashion because
they are always dressing in the same black clothes and putting a cross here. They have no chance to follow new fashions.

And people are running after fashions and practicing what Shaytan is making them to do and to follow. And they are saying, "Your honor is with your clothes. You must take more care of your clothes."

It is written in holy books, and it is traditional knowledge reaching to me, also, from a thousand years ago, about Imam al-Ghazali, a famous learned person, well-known in Western countries as well as in the Islamic world. Western people say that he is the most important philosopher in Islam. Oriental people, Muslims, say, "One of our highest level learned ones, 'alim, a learned person."

He was saying that when a person dies and is put in his coffin and taken to the graveyard, on the way, his Lord, the Lord of Creation, the Lord of the Heavens, Allah Almighty, He will ask him, up to the time his coffin reaches the graveyard, forty questions—before questioning in the grave,[174] forty questions. Imam al-Ghazali was mentioning the first of those questions and keeping thirty-nine to himself.

First, Allah Almighty will ask His servant, "O My servant, I looked at you, and during your life you took perfect care of your outward appearance. As much as possible, you took care of it. You took such care of yourself, of your outward appearance, because you were very happy that people looked at you and said, 'Oh, such beautiful a one!' Some others might say, 'Such a handsome one!' Throughout your whole life, you were interested only in tandhif,[175] decorating

---

[174]It is an Islamic belief that the souls of the dead will be questioned in their graves.

[175]Being well-groomed, well-tended.

your outside appearance so that people might look [and say,] 'O-oh!'

"You took all your care that people would look at you, to see that you are in perfect condition, people appreciating it. And did you ever think about Me, that My gaze was on your heart, to say that my Lord is not looking at our outer being, our forms, but He is looking at our hearts. Did you ever think about it? Have you ever tried to make My gaze reach you while you looked perfect, and to look and to be happy with your heart, that you were taking care of it? Have you ever thought about it?"

That is enough. What people, they are doing for themselves, for their physical being, it is nothing, going to be rubbish with a bad smell. You should be put under the ground in your grave and covered with earth; but your soul, your heart, if you do not take any care of it, Allah Almighty should 'atb, blame you. "O My servant, why were you not taking care about Me, to make a good showing for Me in your heart? Did you ever think of it?"

Now people, all of them are dressing their physical being; so many bad habits, bad fashions. They are saying "new fashions," and they are running after them. They are not running to make their hearts clean, prepared only for their Lord.

We are speaking about knowledge. This is a knowledge that people must know. It is a kind of knowledge that gives honor to its possessor, making his rank over the ranks of common people, making his rank a special rank just different from other people's levels. That gives them honor.

Therefore, the Prophet ﷺ was saying that the highest degree of our ranks, it is not granted to you from the earth, from people. What is granted from the Heavens and what you have dressed on yourself, that is much more, and that is what Allah Almighty is asking His servants to reach. And when His servants are cleaning themselves and coming, they are suitable for heavenly ranks. Then Allah Almighty is dressing them in heavenly ranks. His servants, they have a right to be dressed in heavenly ranks, real ranks, not like the common people living on earth who are asking for ranks and honors from their clothing.

May Allah forgive us and bless you. For the honor of the most honored one in His Divine Presence, Sayyidina Muhammad ﷺ—*bi-hurmati-l-Fateha*. ▲

19

SHAYTAN'S ORIGINAL AIM

A'udhu bil-Lahi min ash-Shaytani-r-rajim. Bismillahi-r-Rahmani-r-Rahim. La haula wa la quwwata illa bil-Lahi-l-'Aliyyi-l-'Adhim. By the name of Allah, All-Mighty, All-Merciful, Most Beneficent and Most Munificent. *Allah-Allah! Ya Allah!*

It is an Association, to give refreshment to our souls. When our souls are getting to be refreshed, then our bodies are becoming open and refreshment is coming to our physical being, because our physical being depends on our spiritual being.

When Allah Almighty created and formed the first man, Adam, the body was lying like a piece of clay. The form was perfect but it couldn't move, couldn't stand up, couldn't see, couldn't hear, couldn't touch, couldn't walk. It was like a piece of rock, you may say, or a statue, nothing else. Then Allah Almighty blew into that one, sending His divine order. 'Blew' means sending His divine order so that the soul came and entered, occupying every part of that form, the form of the new creature, beginning from its head, entering and running through it.

When running through it, it was changing. The secret of life was running into that clay form, running, coming to his eyes, and he was opening his eyes, beginning to see.

Running down through his nose and *aksırmaya, haçu,* sneezing; quickly running to his mouth, and he was saying, *"Alhamdulillah!"* with his *lisan,* tongue, the secret of life running through his tongue, becoming alive, and then going downward. And then standing up—standing up.

That means that our physical being is never going to be something, a living something, if that heavenly support does not reach us. When reaching, then we are standing up, our physical being is standing up. If not, if it is taken from it, falling down; falling down, and going back to its original elements, going back to dust. Therefore, spiritual power makes all people to stand up and to live. When spiritual power reaches from the spiritual world, it makes you to be a living one on earth.

I was seeing on some roads, road work. There is a sign, "Road work," and I saw that there are some lights flashing. Those lamps, it is impossible to stop during the daytime and to begin at nighttime; they are flashing as long as they have capacity to flash. However many days or however many hours, they must flash till finishing. No need of renewal; no renewal for them. They must continue till finishing, and different sizes, different times are just given for those lamps and can't be stopped. When finishing, no renewal— finished. You can't use it a second time; you must throw it away.

You, O mankind, everyone—we have been granted that power, and it is written on it that this should work, should flash, for three days, three months, three years, thirty years, fifty years, eighty years, ninety years; written on it. No one can stop it, no one can renew it. No.

Now, our flash power, spiritual power, it is given, granted, according to divine wisdoms or divine will, to that, to this, to everyone, and it is continuing. But you must know that each breath is making it less, making your time, that we call *ajal*,[176] the time of your life on earth less, less, less, less. Perhaps one million flashes for someone, coming down, coming down, coming down, finishing, finishing, coming to the point of zero.

Our Headquarters is warning people, warning all proud ones who think they can do everything as they like with their powers, and instead of doing their best for people, they are trying to do their worst because their egos like it. And ego belongs to Shaytan. He has [a thirst for] revenge, he has a desire to make mankind to be down, to suffer, to be finished, every moment not to be happy, to be always in troubles, to live through endless problems.

That is Shaytan's main goal, [the reason] why he asked Allah Almighty to leave him up to the Day of Resurrection,[177] why he asked to give trouble, to give sufferings and miseries to mankind. His first aim, that up to today has never changed, is to make mankind to be ground under the mills of two stones, not to live freely and happily and peacefully. That is Shaytan's first and last will. And Allah Almighty was saying, "Go! If you can do that, do anything [you like].![178] If mankind, if the children of Adam, are not listening to My orders and are following you, that is going

---

[176] Appointed time or date, moment of death; also, delay, respite.

[177] 7:14, 15:36, 17:62, 38:79.

[178] Referring to 17:64-65.

to be the punishment for them because they are leaving My heavenly orders and asking to follow you, and I am saying I am going to punish them here and Hereafter. Go!"

Who is the representative, Shaytan's representative, in a person? Ego. Your ego represents Shaytan in yourself. If you are able to use that ego, ego is going to help you to reach higher positions, levels, in the Divine Presence. But if you do not use it [for that] and leave your ego to follow shaytanic commands, shaytanic tricks and shaytanic traps that are put for mankind, you should be punished.

Don't say, "Why does Allah Almighty give us that ego?" O people who are asking such a foolish question, there is an answer from the Seal of the Prophets. The Prophet ﷺ was saying, "Nafsuka matiyatuka."[179] You must know that it is your mount, to ride on and to reach your goals, here and hereafter.

If, for example, I give a ride to a person who hasn't a ride and is carrying his load on his shoulder, and he asks me, "Why are you giving me a ride? I don't need it," he must be foolish, a completely foolish one. How? It is a grant from me to you. I am granting to you a ride. Ride on it and put your load on it, and go on your way! But you are getting angry with me. What is that foolishness? Most people are saying, "For what is ego, nafs? Why is it given to us? He knows that 'Inna-n-nafsa la amaratun bi-s-sou.'[180] Nafs is not good; nafs is from Shaytan, Shaytan's representative. Why does He give it to us? To make us fall into the Fire?"

---

[179]"Your ego is your mount."

[180]"Indeed, the ego is a persistent enjoiner of evil." (12:53)

No. It is given to you to take your heavy load and to let you rest, as you are using mounts on earth. But your ego is just going to be used for your heavenly journey, as the Prophet was granted a journey to the Heavens; and really he was not in need of a Buraq to ride on, but Allah Almighty is teaching everyone *why*, showing people how they should be able to reach heavenly stations in His Divine Presence.

That Buraq was just sent to Rasul-Allah ﷺ: "Ride on it and show a way to your nation, that they can't come to Me without riding on their horses, on their egos." When egos are going to be mounts for us and make us reach to the King of Kings, *Sultan* of *Sultans*, Allah Almighty, and we will ask to come into His Divine Presence, it will be said by guardians who are stationed at that limit, and only they are permitted to come into the Divine Presence; an announcement will come: "Let My servant leave his mount and come to Me." Have you ever seen a person coming to a king's palace, to a *sultan's* palace, riding and asking to come into his royal presence on his mount? What is that? Leave your mount and come!

That means, that is our mount. We must use it till we are reaching to the appointed level for ourselves in the Divine Presence. Then that will leave you and you are free with your Lord, Almighty Allah. But *nafs*, that represents Shaytan, it is not a true one. Its characteristic just has a different structure. Man's mount, man's ego, it is just a hundred per cent different from every creature, and its characteristic is so bad.

What is was Shaytan's aim when Allah Almighty ordering to make *sajdah*, to bow to Adam, and everyone from the *malaika, angels were* quickly bowing? He said, "I am not making *sajda* to him." What was his purpose in refusing? To sit on the station of glory, *"Maqam al-mahmoud,"* [181] and to be instead of Sayyidina Muhammad ﷺ in the top position of whole creation. That was his thinking or intention, because that honor just going to be only for one, that you are calling *"Maqam al-mahmoud."* Allah Almighty saying, that is the most glorified station, the throne that anyone from creatures can reach; but it is only for one, and it is for the Seal of Prophets, the most honored one in the Divine Presence, Sayyidina Muhammad ﷺ.

It was so easy for Shaytan to bow, but he was asking to be that most glorified, *mahmoud,* and praised station through creation, to be for him, to be there instead of the Prophet, *astaghfirullah.* That is what his struggling and arguing with Allah Almighty, not for *sajdah.* He was putting this, "You created that one from earth, I am created from the flame of fire," [but] don't think it was so simple a thing—no. Behind, behind, behind, *awliwa* they are knowing. Without opening his mouth, it was well known. *"Ala y'alamu man khalaq?"*[182] Allah Almighty not knowing what He created, what that asking? Yes, knowing. Therefore, he is arguing in front of angels to save himself, to bring a proof, saying, "I am better; I am from the flame of fire, while this one is from earth." It is so simple.

No need for arguing. Who asked him if he was created from the flame of fire? Allah did not know? Allah knew!. And that Adam was created from earth? *He* created him;

---

[181]The praiseworthy station to which Allah Almighty promised to raise His Last Messenger (17:79).

[182]*"Does He who created not know?"* (67:14)

not knowing? But his secret [desire] was to be, on behalf of Allah Almighty, all glory be for Him, the highest of all creation. Therefore he was kicked out.

And Shaytan and ego, they are on the same line. They want, ego wants, to be the representative of Shaytan. And when Shaytan lost that—because it was not for him, it was for Adam ﷺ —he was arguing and beginning to make trouble.

When he was beginning to make trouble, the divine order came: "Kick him down! Kick him down! He can't speak in My Divine Presence in such a way. Kick him down!" And He was saying, "Demon! Devil! Take away his outside appearance that I dressed on him, an honored dressing— take it and leave him to be the ugliest one among My creatures!" And he was kicked down.

Therefore, he was asking to be with mankind up to the end, the Day of Resurrection. "Go!"[183] For what? To take his revenge from mankind through their egos, using the egos of mankind, and he is making, every time, trouble. The first trouble-maker, up to the end, is Shaytan, and his representatives. Now, fully all the people on this planet, all of them are trouble-makers.

"I am not making trouble."

I am asking, "Are you praying?"

"No."

"You are the first trouble-maker. Your line is Shaytan's line because he was ordered to make sajdah, to prostrate,

---

[183]4:118-119, 7:16-17, 15:39-40, 38:82-83, 17:64-

and he did not move. You, also, five times a day, Allah Almighty is ordering you to prostrate in His Divine Presence and you are not doing [even] one of those.

Trouble-makers are under the command of Shaytan, and you are never going to be happy, here or Hereafter. Now, everyone, everyone among the twenty-first century's people, everyone is a trouble-maker. How are you asking to bring peace on earth with such foolish inhabitants—how, while everyone, according to his size, is a trouble-maker? From king-sized ones down to ant-sized ones, everyone is making trouble, to give people *adha*,[184] to hurt people, to give to people *asaf*, sorrow; sorrow-makers and trouble-makers, and another word, also. They are wild people, horrible people; they are happy to hurt people, to kill people, to destroy people, to destroy their cultures, to destroy their homes, to destroy their villages, to destroy their buildings. All of them are Shaytan's representatives.

Everyone now is a trouble-maker. Therefore, everyone must be taken away. That divine order is just in action now. From the beginning of 1425,[185] it is going on. Impossible, peace; till Mahdi ﷺ comes, and one of the biggest representatives of Shaytan, the Anti-Christ,[186]comes, and Jesus Christ comes and kills that biggest trouble-maker after Shaytan, and then peace *yastaqir*, will be established, on earth. If not, finished, this world.

---

[184]Harm.

[185]The *Hijri* (Islamic) calendar year.

[186]That is, the Dajjal (Arch-Deceiver), the False Messiah whose coming and actions are foretold in many *hadiths*.

Keep yourself away from those, Shaytan's representatives. Leave them to eat each other! As long as they do not fear Allah Almighty, let them kill each other, destroy each other. Never-ending troubles and sufferings for them! It is true for them.

May Allah forgive us. And may Allah send us what we are hoping, hoping for—Mahdi 舜 to come quickly and to save even one handful of believers, and it is enough for even a handful of believers and good ones to stay on earth, just as there rode on the Ark of Noah eighty people, and the others were all drowned, finished, Allah giving a new generation from eighty people.

Now, there are going to be many more people remaining [on earth], but the majority should be drowned, should be burned, should be destroyed. Not any system, not any state or states, can stop it. It is a divine punishment because that the earth's people now are making their leader Shaytan and following him. As long as they do not change their ways, all of them are going to fall into Hells here and hereafter.

May Allah forgive us and grant you from His endless Mercy Oceans. For the honor of the most honored one in His Divine Presence—*Fateha.* ▲

20

MERCY RAINFALL FROM HEAVEN

A'udhu bil-Lahi min ash-Shaytani-r-rajim. Bismillahi-r-Rahmani-r-Rahim. La haula wa la quwwata illa bil-Lahi-l-'Aliyyi-l-'Adhim.

It is an Association. We are asking Allah Almighty, from His endless Mercy Oceans, to send to us.

One day, the Seal of the Prophets, the most honored one in the Divine Presence, Sayyidina Muhammad ﷺ, he was coming home to his holy, perhaps the holiest place, on earth—coming, and Sayyidatina 'A'isha,[187] Allah bless her, was coming and looking at the Prophet, doing like this [surveying him]. And the Prophet was asking, "Why you are doing this, O 'A'isha?"

"Because there was heavy rain and I was worried about you, O most honored one, most beloved one in the Divine Presence, if you were wet under that heavy rain."

The Prophet was saying, *"Subhanallah,* glory be to Allah!"

---

[187]The Prophet's wife.

"And I am seeing that there is nothing on you, no wetness."

And Sayyidina Rasul-Allah ﷺ, the most praised one in the Divine Presence, was asking, "O 'A'isha, what was on your head at that time?"

And she answered, "Your cover, scarf."

[He said,] "And that made you see something that belongs to spirituality that surrounds this world. Your putting that scarf on your head was just an opening to you to see that another kind of rain is always raining on earth."

It is true. It is not that ordinary rain that you know—no. Ordinary rain gives life to the whole material world, giving life to those living on earth and in oceans, also.

Some people, they may ask what is the benefit of clouds raining on the sea, on oceans. Everything coming from above gives life; every atom is in need of heavenly mercy to live and to continue their lives, even in oceans. And traditional knowledge reaching to ourselves [informs us] that angels are bringing rain from Heavens on earth.

We are not philosophers, to follow their foolish idea that rain is coming from the seas, going up, *tabakhkhur*, evaporation. They are saying that water, seas, are sending up vapor, going up and becoming clouds, and from clouds—*wsh-h!*—[rains are coming automatically].[188] I am

---

[188]According to Islamic tradition, the dispensation of rain is in the charge of the archangel Michael ﷺ (Mika'il). In Christian, Jewish and other traditions, Michael ﷺ is also the archangel in charge of nature: clouds, rain, snow, lightning and thunder.

saying, "*Yahu*, can you carry a container with one gallon of water? Are you able to take it up and send it down?"

What is that? How can it be? And they are saying that a cloud carrying *rahmat-Allah*,[189] carrying rain, a middle-sized or small-sized cloud, carries 300,000 tons of water.

They are knowing and saying this. Then they are saying that this is coming up from oceans. How? No-mind people. They are ashamed to say that Allah Almighty sends rains, coming from the Heavens, angels bringing it down. Yes! Those rains are giving to everything on earth that belongs to our material world, giving it life. *"Wa ja'alna mina-l-ma'a kulla shayin hayy."*[190]

The secret of life is in water. If no water, no life. And you are coming from a drop of water—not a gallon of water, no; only one drop; another kind of water. It is not a solid thing, no; it is a kind of water, also. From one drop of water a person comes. Our physical being just comes through that one drop of extraordinary water or the most distinguished water on earth—most distinguished water. Other waters, they give trees, plants, life, but it is a special water that makes you to come into life and to be prepared to carry the heavenly *amanat*, trust. Therefore, it is an other, special and most distinguished water.

They are trying to find what is in it. They can't see. They are making so many theories and saying "DNA." DNA, in Turkish, is *dana*. *Dana* means a calf. Calf—DNA.

---

[189] Allah's mercy, beneficence, compassion—that is, the rain that sustains all things on earth.

[190] *"And We made every living thing from water."* (21:30)

Europeans can't say it, and they are saying "Dee-eN-Ay". Our people can say "DANA."

"Did you look at your DANA?"

"Not yet. I will enter a machine to see which kind of DANA I come from."

The special, most special, most distinguished, the secret of your personality, the secrets of your living physical body that is commanded and *idare*,[191] directed and controlled, through your unknown personality that does not belong to your physical being [is in that extraordinary water]. That rain, ordinary rain, comes for your physical being, and all things in this material world are taking their shares, shares for their lives. But it [rain] is not enough to continue the lives of people. The lives of people on earth, they are in need of some other kind of rain that can't be seen by ordinary eyes. It needs some extraordinary eyes that belong to our real personality in our hearts, to look and to see. Those whose hearts are closed, their eyes blind in their hearts, they can't see. And that rain is for supporting the life of mankind on this planet, and everything is in need of that rain, also. If not coming, no energy will reach you through your eating and drinking. That special rain must rain on all things; all things must take their shares.

We are in need and we are asking from our Lord, Almighty Allah, to send us some of His lions that are special, they have a special creation—to send to us for directing all things on earth, because now all things are just passing out

---

[191]Directed, managed, administered.

of their orbit, and it is a dangerous direction that mankind is hastening towards, running faster, faster, faster to that bad end.

And we were beginning to say—They are making me to address you for a [specific] occasion—that that rain was also coming on prophets, at the top level, and also, for prophets' levels, becoming more and more. Then, when they passed away, their inheritors [awliya], they were appointed for those Mercy Oceans' rains, heavenly rains. And always we are asking for a beloved one in His Divine Presence, to reach to him, or he may reach to our meeting, to our assembly, jama'at, gathering, so then they are carrying more of that special rain.

I am happy to say that Shaykh Mustafa is coming today, and I was happy that, through his spirituality, those rains are coming on us. Therefore, today is just honored with such a special servant. You saw him, you may recognize him. Maybe you know only "Shaykh Mustafa," but maybe his personality in the spiritual world is just different and brings power to our meetings. Therefore, meetings, their value is according to attenders. The one whose *himmet*, aspiration, is high may bring more divine rains on us. Therefore—Allah-Allah! *Subhanallah!*—we have been ordered in the Holy Qur'an, *"Wa kunu m'aa-s-sadiqin"*[192]—to ask for such people who are true to their Lord, to be with them, so that you may reach at every moment a new refreshment from heavenly rains.

---

[192] *"And be with those who are true."* (9:119)

Now people, they have, all of them, no life. Their lives are only material lives, and material life, it is only as if three months ago, everywhere it was green. Now all fields they are dry; only trees they are keeping their greenness because their creation is just different. And people, also, mostly they are like grass; for a short while they may be green, giving pleasure, and in a short time they are disappearing. But trees—trees, their beauty, their lives, are going on. For grass [and other annual plants], you must renew its planting every year, but not for trees, each year cutting and putting a new tree there, no. They grow [continuously]. According to our situation [on this planet,] it is enough. Therefore, in Paradise, trees are growing, getting more bright and giving more pleasure to Paradise-people. No need to renew, but growing and granting all the time more pleasure to people.

Therefore, *aqil*, perfect-minded, people are asking to follow—to ask, to search for such people whose refreshment is continuing and they are carrying mercy from the Heavens. That is the reason that Allah Almighty is ordering, "O My servants, run to such people whose refreshment, whose lights never become less but increase. If you would like to be happy here and Hereafter, follow those ones. Don't ask for a refreshment or shelter from grass. [Plants like] grasses never continue their refreshment and they can't shelter you, but trees can."

O people, now the whole world is in its most terrible days, as we are informed in prophets' speeches and their addressing to people. They are giving news of the Last Day, when it is coming, what it should be. It is written, but people are so foolish, even the Muslim world more than others, not opening those books that contain the signs of Last Day, and they are running like drunk peoplen to save themselves by themselves.

Can't be! They are not asking for a heavenly shelter, heavenly salvation; they are not asking, "O our Lord, save our souls!" No! They are running like foolish ones, crazy ones, drunk ones and heedless ones, asking to arrange the world and everything in it. Each day, newspapers and those Shaytan-boxes[193] are showing and saying that all of *dunya* is just in the hands of terrorism, while terrorists, if you collect them, they are not going to be more than 100,000 or 200,000 or one million. All, everyone, they are trembling. Why not running to good ones? If bad ones are threatening you, go—run to good ones who have power from the Heavens. Terrorists may have their power from shaytanic ways on earth, but true ones, they are supported by heavenly powers. Why are you not running to *them*?

No! Grinding them now; they should die. Everything that they built on behalf of Shaytan should be destroyed. Everyone who is living for Shaytan should be taken away. Those who are living for Allah should stay, and Allah Almighty should give them an inheritor on earth up to the appointed time for the Last Day.

May Allah grant that inspiration to run to good ones. Still people are not running, not asking for true ones and good ones; still they are running from one bad one to another, worse one. May Allah forgive us and protect us. For the honor of the most honored one in His Divine Presence— *Fateha.* ▲

---

[193]Television.

21

WITHOUT SPIRITUAL POWER NOTHING MOVES

A'udhu bil-Lahi min ash-Shaytani-r-rajim. Bismillahi-r-Rahmani-r-Rahim. La haula wa la quwwata illa bil-Lahi-l-'Aliyyi-l-'Adhim.

It is an Association, and for our physical being it is a support because association gives spiritual support to our physical being, and [at the same time] association addresses our spirituality. When your spirituality gets happy, it gives much more support to your physical being. If you do not take care of your spirituality, normally your physical being always goes down, down, down, and finishes.

This is a recorder. It works in two ways. One, you may use it with a battery, *pil*. But also it has two holes. You may use a wire, putting the central electricity, and from the central electricity comes power and it works as long as this central electricity works. But if you using *pils*, you may use it till that *pil* finishes, and *pils'* power also slowly, slowly comes down, becoming less and less.

Therefore, a person may use his physical being, and he is trusting in his physical being's working, and he is running and trying to do something. And in their youth time it is okay; he thinks that he will never be in need of any other power. He feels that his physical being it is okay, and according to his understanding, he can run like a horse, he can carry heavy loads like a donkey, and he can jump with high jumps like a chimpanzee, monkey, and he is very proud. Oh, ho-ho-ho-ho-ho-ho! Oh, first class, first class athlete!

[Parodies:] They are preparing for Olympics in Athens. For the first time, I went and looked at such a place. In the year 1836, that ampitheatre was begun. It was, at the beginning, at first, for 80,000 people, ;

I was standing there, I was saying, "Take a photograph, that Shaykh, also, now he is first." No one was there. "The first medal for Shaykh to be here, before others, athletes, running people, particularly our African brothers—oh-ho-ho-ho! No one can reach to them."

"From where are you learning?" I was asking [the athletes].

"From a cheetah, running." They were saying, "We learned to run by looking at cheetahs. Running," they were saying, "we learned from our countries, and no one can reach to us. Yes. Jumping, we are learning from apes, jumping from tree to tree, high jumps." And faster than that *nakıshlı arslan*,[194] they are learning from them. They are very happy when they are getting first [place], and they are not using these heavy things [weights], to lift it up, like this, like this, weight-lifting champion. They are not interested in such things. White people are very much interested in this. *Yahu*, this is much better. They look like horses, but the ones who are carrying heavy loads look like donkeys.

---

[194]Decorated lion.

Everyone—*suhanallahi-l-'Aliyyi-l-'Adhim*, glory be to Allah Almighty!—is running to show his powers, and all of it, it is youth power, up to a level. After that level, your physical being no more gives you support. That comes down, comes down, and finishes.

Real support for our physical being that is never cut off, it is from our spiritual power. If that gives you support, you should be powerful and keep your youth power as it was when you were fifteen years, while you may be ninety years. But people now, they think that physical being can be supported only by material things. Yes; asking power from their physical being, and they are using material things to give more support to their physical being. That is never going to be useful, but making it to come down. Spirituality can take you up.

A plane can fly. It does not fly by material things, no. That material is changing into another state that can fly. If you put that petrol into a plane, if you want that petrol to make it fly as it is, it can't be. That petrol changes its state, becoming another material, but it is not a material that can be seen. No, you can't touch it. When you are putting that petroleum into a plane, you can touch it. But when it goes up, you can't touch it, that power just changing into another form that is going to be like a spiritual being for that plane and making it to fly.[195]

Therefore, we, if we are not asking our physical being to be changed through our spiritual power, you can't reach real power to do something for heavenly aspects, or to reach

---

[195]The meaning here is that although material objects may use material means to function, the reality behind what powers their functioning is actually spiritual.

peace, to reach hope, to reach a good position, a better condition. If you are not using your spirituality, you can't reach real aspects and never-ending powers; you can't reach.

Now, people, they are not thinking about such aspects, but really we are in need of that. We need support, spiritual support, personally and generally. People now, in the twenty-first century, they are not asking for that support; they think that material powers are enough for them. But it is never going to be enough. You must use heavenly powers, whose stations are very rare. But if you are asking, you can find someone who leads you or guides you to those power stations.

All *awliya*, who are inheritors of prophets, they are heavenly power stations on earth. If you reach to them, then they may give you that power to make you reach your heavenly stations; otherwise, you can't fly to those stations by planes, by rockets, by missiles and such things—no, no. Perhaps most or all of them, they may go up a little bit, then turn back down, no more able to carry people to high stations in the Heavens. And men, they are in need to reach the Heavens because Allah Almighty just granted to His servants a private seat, a private station, to be there.

You must ask how I can reach, with whom I can reach. If a person does not use a plane, he can't move even from one side to another side of this world. He begins and ends on earth. What about if you want to reach your heavenly stations, from which you are asking not to come back? You should be happy there because you should be dressed in the dress of honor of being servants, for divine service in His Divine Presence, that glorious station giving to you glory never-ending.

People they are drunk now, drunk with their material [things], and their trust is only in material aspects. They think that material [things] can support them for their every aim, but finally they are looking and seeing that their material [supports] can't reach them, aren't able to support them. There may come a kind of virus into that person who was thinking that he is powerful and he is the richest one, or he is in the highest position in his nation.

They are thinking that such [material] things should help them. And Allah Almighty is sending a virus—a virus, and that person is looking for help from his soldiers, but soldiers can't help him. Asking from his missiles, "Help me!" They are saying, "We can't!" Asking from his gold, "Help me!" It is saying, "We can't!" Asking from his jewels, "Help me against that virus! I am so weak in front of that unseen virus."

A person was with a king, sitting; he was a heavenly-supported person. And the king was sitting on his throne. Allah Almighty wanted to show something to that king, and let a fly [loose on him], coming there, doing like this. Running away; coming again; doing like this, doing like this, but the fly never went away.

He was so angry and restless, and he said, "For what are these flies?"

And that spiritually-powerful person said, "Oh! Command them, order them, to go away."

And he was saying, "I can't!"

And he was saying, "If you are so weak that you aren't able to send away flies, how you are claiming that I am such a powerful one, keeping in one of your hands an orb, in one hand your sword, and on your head a crown, and even flies are never listening, never obeying you? Why you are going to be there, sitting, so proud a person?" Yes.

This is a small fly. Smaller, as I said, is a virus. It may come. Calling all doctors, physicians, and saying, "Help me! Help me and I shall give to you everything."

And they are saying, "I tried everything for you, but we can't do anything more." No one is helping! If not asking help from saints, who are the *sultans* of *akhirat*, *sultans* of the eternal life—if you are not going to look for them and to see them, to find them, and to ask help from them, your rank, your richness, your soldiers, your atomic bombs, your nuclear bombs, your aircraft will never help you, O man. Don't be proud; come down! Prostrate to Allah! Ask help from Him.

If you are asking how can we reach to asking [help] from Him, we may say, "You must look for those people who are His servants—*His servants*." They have such a power to help you. They may take everything that *t'ajiz*,[196] is hurting you, harming you; they may help you, they may take everything from you."

Then that *wali* was saying, "Look, O king! I am ordering. O flies, get out!" There was a hole, and then, one by one, they were going, going, going, going out. "You are the *sultan* or I am the *sultan*? Look! Flies are never obeying your order but obeying *my* order. Because I am His servant,

---

[196]Also, worrying, bothering, harassing.

they must obey me. But you are claiming you are not a servant; you are claiming that I am king, I am not a servant. Therefore they are not obeying you."

Yes, welcome to you. Everything teaches people, but people they are drunk, running after Shaytan and shaytanic teachings, never giving a way for them to learn heavenly knowledge. They are taking away heavenly knowledge, traditional knowledge, thrown out of universities, academies and such places. All shaytanic teachings are in them, and shaytanic teachings are bringing people at the edge of these cliffs. They should fall into the fire.

May Allah forgive me and bless you. For the honor of the most honored one in His Divine Presence, Sayyidina Muhammad 🕌—*Fateha*. ▲

22

THE POWER OF *TARIQAT* AGAINST DEPRESSION

Since *himmah* is down after 'Isha, I don't like to make a full Association. Also, some guests are leaving tomorrow.

For every beginning there should be an end: this life is just based on that rule. Every meeting is ended by a separation, every separation comes to a meeting, and every meeting comes to a separation.

For so many days our visitors have been with us. They have come for the love of Allah. They are asking for peace and happiness and to be more obedient; they have felt in need of new spiritual power to help against egos and devils. And I hope that in coming, Allah is granting them something of peace and satisfaction. I am asking from Allah not to take back their happiness and refreshment; that they may travel back to their homeland, and that in every meeting when they are with people, they may transfer this happiness and peace to others by their words and good condition, physical and otherwise.

It is important for everyone to reach to these good feelings and extend them to others who may be in bad conditions or depression. A man may be sick, and when you understand that he is seriously sick, maybe terminal, you may say, "There is a specialist for cure in a distant city," and that person will run after that specialist for his health.

Now millions are in depression, and it will cover more and more. It is still on the rise because conditions are helping and the conditions favoring depression are expanding. You [the guests who are leaving] may say, "We were in such a condition and tried ways which have saved us from this condition." That is important so that you may give benefit to mankind.

I am asking that Allah continues your peace and satisfaction in your hearts forever. It is one of the holiest months—first this month, then another, and then Ramadan. Ramadan is the holiest of the months, and all may reach to peace in that holy month.

You must make 'advertising' for Sufi ways, especially for the Most Distinguished Naqshbandi Way. It isn't difficult; it is easy, reaching to the first station, then to the station of Gabriel, 安 and after the station of Gabriel 安, our minds may understand something.

Gabriel 安 represents mind, 'aql. After Gabriel 安, our minds stop. After that, we can't use our mind for understanding; our mind is finished. That is the beginning of the Naqshbandi Way.

Forty tariqats are taking people to the Station of Gabriel 安; that is their end. But for the Most Distinguished Naqshbandi Tariqat, it is the beginning. The Most Distinguished Naqshbandi Tariqat reaches people and carries them to the highest levels; all other tariqats are only preparing people for the Naqshbandi Way. It belongs to [Abu

Bakr] as-Siddiq,[197] as-Siddiq to the Prophet, and the Prophet directly to Allah.

If you are with a person, you must look after him, and later you may say something to him as advice. Don't say from the first day, "I am calling you to Islam."

Try it on yourself, step by step. Don't say "Islam," say "the Sufi way." Whoever accepts Sufi ways is accepting Islam but you needn't say so. The *Shari'ah* is like a huge bridge from your ego to Paradise. Can you accept the castle without accepting the bridge?

You must use wisdoms for yourself and for other people. But people never understand in our time. Everyone is asking for investment; people are carrying too- materialistic ideas. Those people are not accepting unless seeing benefit.

Depressed people may reach benefit in three days, some in one week, some in three weeks, some in one month, some in forty days. They may reach to important bases to protect them from the devil.

Take a [shower] bath, and after all are sleeping, you may sit in a silent and dark place and be with yourself for ten minutes.

Don't be afraid! The one who is speaking to you is your ego. No fear; when doing such a practice, you are beginning to use will power. After three nights, you should reach to strong will power.

---

[197]The close Companion of the Prophet, the first caliph of Islam.

Therefore, you must return to your homelands, and don't run away from people. You may be with society and with people. You may ask permission from Grandshaykh, and even if entering the army and they are all against you, if there is permission from Grandshaykh, no worry. One after the other, you may give benefit, and no material system or all material systems are successful for curing depression except all *tariqats*, Islamic mysticism, and the Naqshbandi Way. ▲

GLOSSARY

Abu Bakr as-Siddiq—the closest of the Prophet's Companions and his father-in-law, who shared the Hijrah with him. After the Prophet's death, he was chosen by consensus of the Muslims as the first caliph or successor to the Prophet. He is known as one of the most saintly of the Prophet's Companions.

'Abdul-Khaliq al-Ghujdawani—the eleventh grandsheikh of the Naqshbandi *tariqah*, one of the Khwajagan of Central Asia.

Abu Hanifa—the founder of one of the four schools of Islamic jurisprudence, the Hanafi *madhhab*.

Abu Yazid Bistami—Bayazid Bistami, a great ninth century *wali* and Naqshbandi master.

Adab—good manners, proper etiquette.

Adhan—the call to prayer.

Ahl al-Bait—People of the House, that is, the family of the Holy Prophet ﷺ.

Ahl ad-dunya—people of the world, i.e., those who are attached to its life and pleasures.

Akhirah—the Hereafter, the Eternal Life.

Alhamdulillah—praise be to Allah, praise God.

Allahu akbar—God is the Most Great.

Amir (pl., 'umara)—chief, leader, head of a nation or people.

Anbiya (plural of **nabi**)—prophets.

'Aql—mind, intellect, intelligence, reason, discernment.

'Arafat—a vast plain outside Mecca where pilgrims gather for the principal rite of Hajj.

'Arif—knower; in the present context, one who has reached spiritual knowledge of his Lord.

Ar-Rahim—the Mercy-Giving, Merciful, Munificent, one of Allah's ninety-nine Holy Names

Ar-Rahman—the Most Merciful, Compassionate, Beneficent, the most often repeated of Allah's Holy Names.

Ashhadu an la ilaha illa-Llah wa ashhadu anna Muhammadu Rasul-Allah—"I bear witness that there is no deity except Allah and I bear witness that Muhammad is Allah's messenger," the Islamic *Shahadah* or Declaration of Faith.

Astaghfirullah—I seek Allah's forgiveness.

A'udhu bil-Lahi min ash-Shaytani-r-Rajim—I seek refuge in Allah from Satan the accursed.

Awliya (sing., **wali**)—the "friends" of Allah, Muslim saints or holy people.

Bait al-Maqdi— the Sacred House in Jerusalem, built atthe site where Solomon's Temple was later erected.

Barakah—blessings.

Batil—vain or false; falsehood, deception.

Bayah—pledge; in the context of this book, the pledge of a disciple (murid) to a sheikh.

Bi-hurmati-l-Fatehah—for the honor or respect of Surat al-Fatehah (the opening chapter of the Qur'an).

Bismillahi-r-Rahmani-r-Rahim— "In the name of Allah, the Beneficent, the Merciful," the invocation with which all a Muslim's actions are supposed to begin.

Dajjal—the False Messiah whom the Prophet 鐢 foretold as coming at the end-time of this world, who will deceive mankind with pretensions of being divine.

Day of Promises—the occasion in the spiritual world when Allah Almighty called together the souls of all human beings to come and asked them to acknowledge His Lordship and sovereignty (7:172).

Dhikr (zikr, zikir)—message, remembrance or reminder, used in the Qur'an to refer to the Qur'an and other revealed scriptures. Dhikr (or dhikr-Allah) also refers to remembering Allah through repetition of His Holy Names or various phrases of glorification (for the meanings of the phrases of dhikr mentioned in this book, see the footnote entries under individual phrases).

Dhulm (zulm)—injustice, oppression, tyranny, misuse, transgressing proper limits, wrong-doing.

Du'a—supplication, personal prayer.

173

Dunya—this world and its attractions, worldly involvements.

Efendi—mister, sir.

'Eid—festival; the two major festivals of Islam are 'Eid al-Fitr, marking the completion of Ramadan, and 'Eid al-Adha, the Festival of Sacrifice during the time of Hajj.

Fard—obligatory, prescribed.

Fard al-kifayah – an obligation which suffices to be met by one or a few persons in a community.

Fatehah—al-Fatehah, the opening surah or chapter of the Qur'an.

Fitnah (pl., **fitan**)—trial, test, temptation; also, discord, dissension.

Grandshaykh—a wali of great stature. In this text, where spelled with a capital "G," "Grandshaykh" refers to Maulana 'Abdullah ad-Daghestani, Shaykh Nazim's shaykh, to whom he was closely attached for forty years up to the time of Grandshaykh's death in 1973.

Hadith (pl., **ahadith**)—a report of the Holy Prophet's sayings, contained in the collections of early hadith scholars. In this text, "Hadith" has been used to refer to the entire body of his oral

traditions, while "hadith" denotes an individual tradition.

Halal—lawful, permissible.

Hajji—one who has performed Hajj, the sacred pilgrimage of Islam.

Halal—permitted, lawful according to the Islamic Shari'ah.

Haqq—truth, reality.

Haram—forbidden, unlawful.

Hasha—God forbid! Never!

Haqq—truth, reality.

Haram—prohibited, unlawful.

Hasan al-Basri – a great scholar of the seventh century C.E.

Hawa—desires, lusts, passions of the lower self or nafs.

Hidayah/hidayat—guidance.

Hijab—barrier, screen, veil or curtain; the covering of Muslim women.

Himmah—desire, zeal, eagerness, ambition, determination.

Hu—the divine pronoun, He.

Ibrahim—the prophet Abraham.

Imam—leader; specifically, the leader of a congregational prayer.

Iman—faith, belief.

Iman—faith, belief.

Insha'Allah – God willing, if God wills.

'Isa—the prophet Jesus ﷺ.

'Isha – night; specifically, the night prayer.

Jababirah—tyrants, oppressors.

Jinn—an invisible order of beings created by Allah from fire.

Kafir—a denier or rejector; in an Islamic context, one who denies Allah (an unbeliever or atheist) or does not acknowledge or is ungrateful for divine favors.

Khalifah—deputy, successor, vicegerent.

Khidr—a holy man, mentioned in the Qur'an, 18:60-82, to whom God has granted life up to the end of the world..

Kufr—unbelief, denial of Allah.

La haula wa la quwwata illa bil-Lah al-'Aliyi-l-'Adhim—"There is no might nor power except in Allah, the Most High, the All-Mighty," words that Muslims utter frequently during their daily lives, signifying total reliance upon Allah.

La ilaha illa-Llah, Muhammadu rasul-Allah—there is no deity except Allah, Muhammad is the Messenger of Allah.

Mahdi—the divinely-appointed guide whose coming at the end-time of this world is mentioned in several authoritative hadiths. He will lead the believers and establish a rule of justice and righteousness for a period of time prior to the events preceding the end of the world and the Last Judgment.

Masha'Allah—what or as Allah willed.

Masjid—literally, a place where sujud, prostration, is made, i.e., a mosque.

Maula—master, lord, protector, patron, referring to Allah Most High.

Me'raj—the Holy Prophet's ascension to the Heavens and the Divine Presenc.

Muezzin—one who makes the call to prayer (adhan).

Muluk (sing., **malik**)—kings, monarchs.

Mumin/muminah—male/female believers in Islam.

Munkar—that which is disapproved, rejected or considered abominable in Islam.

Murid—a disciple or follower of a shaykh.

Murshid—spiritual guide, pir.

Musa—the prophet Moses ﷺ.

Muwahhid – one who proclaims the Unity of Allah Almighty.

Nafs—(1) soul, self, person; (2) the lower self, the ego.

Nasihah—good advice or counsel, admonition, reminder.

Nur—light.

Qada wa qadar—the sixth pillar of Islamic faith, referring to the divine decree.

Qiblah—direction; specifically, the direction of Mecca.

Qisas—retaliation.

Qiyamat/Qiyamah—the Day of Resurrection.

Rabi'ah al-Adawiyah—Rabi'ah Basri, a great womansaint of the eighth century C.E.

Rabitah—bond, connection, tie, link, in the context of this book, with a shaykh.

Rak'at—a cycle or unit of the Islamic prayer (salat), which is repeated a specified number of times in each prayer.

Ramadan—the ninth month of the Islamic lunar calendar, the month of fasting.

Rasul-Allah—the Messenger of God, Muhammad ﷺ.

Sahabah (sing., sahabi)—the Companions of the Prophet, the first Muslims.

Sajdah (also sujud)—prostration.

Salat—the prescribed Islamic prayer or worship.

Sallallahu 'alayhi was-salam—the Islamic invocation on the Prophet ﷺ, meaning, "May Allah's peace and blessings be upon him."

Salawat—invoking blessings and peace upon the Holy Prophet ﷺ.

Sayyid—leader; also, a descendant of the Holy Prophet.

Sayyidina—our chief, master.

Sayyidina 'Ali—the cousin and son-in-law of the Prophet 鸞 and the fourth caliph of Islam.

Sayyidina 'Umar—'Umar ibn al-Khattab, the Prophet's eminent Companion and the second caliph of Islam.

Shahadah—the Islamic creed or Declaration of Faith, "Ash-shadu an la ilaha illa-Llah wa ashhadu anna Muhammu rasul Allah, I bear witness that there is no deity except Allah and I bear witness that Muhammad is His messenger."

Shah Naqshband—Grandshaykh Muhammad Bahauddin Shah-Naqshband, a great eighth century wali, the founder of the Naqshbandi Tariqah.

Shari'at/Shari'ah—the divine Law of Islam, based on the Qur'an and the Sunnah of the Prophet 鸞.

Shirk—polytheism, ascribing divinity or divine attributes to anything other than God.

Shaykh Sharafuddin—the shaykh of Grandshaykh 'Abdullah ad-Daghistani.

Shaytan—Satan.

Sohbet (Arabic, **suhbah**)—a shaykh's talk or discourse ("Association").

Subhanallah—glory be to Allah.

Sultan al-Awliya—lit., "the king of the awliya,' the highest ranking saint.

Sunnah—the practice of the Holy Prophet; that is, what he did, said, recommended or approved of in his Companions. In this text, "Sunnah" is used to refer to the collective body of his actions, sayings or recommendations, while "sunnah" refers to an individual action or recommendation.

Surah—chapter of the Qur'an.

Takbir—the pronouncement of God's greatness, "Allahu akbar, God is Most Great."

Tarawih—the special nighly prayers of Ramadan.

Tariqah/tariqat—literally, way, road or path. An Islamic order or path of discipline and devotion under the guidance of a shaykh (*pir, wali*); Islamic Sufism.

Tawaf—the rite of circumambulatin the K'abah while glorifying Allah, one of the rites of Hajj and 'Umrah.

'Ulama (sing, **'alim**)—scholars, specifically of Islam.

'Umar—see Sayyidina 'Umar.'

Ummah—faith community, nation.

'Umrah—the minor pilgrimage to Mecca, which can be performed at any time of the year.

Uns – familiarity.

Wali (pl., **awliya**)—a Muslim holy man or saint.

Wa min Allah at-taufiq—And success is only from Allah.

Wudu—the prescribed minor ablution preceding prayers and other acts of worship.

Ya Rabb—O Lord.

Zakat/zakah—the obligatgory charity of Islam, one of its five "pillars" or acts of worship.

Zakat al-Fitr—the obligatory charity of 'Eid al-Fitr, the festival marking the completion of Ramadan.

Other titles from

INSTITUTE FOR SPIRITUAL & CULTURAL ADVANCEMENT

Online ordering available from www.isn1.net

The Path to Spiritual Excellence
By Shaykh Muhammad Nazim Adil al-Haqqani
ISBN 1-930409-18-4, Paperback. 180 pp.

This compact volume provides practical steps to purify the heart and overcome the destructive characteristics that deprive us of peace and inner satisfaction. On this amazing journey doubt, fear, and other negative influences that plague our lives - and which we often pass on to our children - can be forever put aside. Simply by introducing in our daily lives those positive thought patterns and actions that attract divine support, we can reach spiritual levels that were previously inaccessible.

In the Mystic Footsteps of Saints
By Shaykh Muhammad Nazim Adil al-Haqqani
Volume 1 - ISBN 1-930409-05-2
Volume 2 – ISBN 1-930409-09-5
Volume 3 – ISBN 1-930409-13-3, Paperback. Ave. length 200 pp.

Narrated in a charming, old-world storytelling style, this highly spiritual series offers several volumes of practical guidance on how to establish serenity and peace in daily life, heal emotional and spiritual scars, and discover the role we are each destined to play in the universal scheme.

Classical Islam and the Naqshbandi Sufi Tradition

By Shaykh Muhammad Hisham Kabbani

ISBN 1-930409-23-0, Hardback. 950 pp.

ISBN 1-930409-10-9, Paperback. 744 pp.

This esteemed work includes an unprecedented historical narrative of the forty saints of the renowned Naqshbandi Golden Chain, dating back to Prophet Muhammad in the early seventh century. With close personal ties to the most recent saints, the author has painstakingly compiled rare accounts of their miracles, disciplines, and how they have lent spiritual support throughout the world for fifteen centuries. Traditional Islam and the Naqshbandi Sufi Tradition is a shining tribute to developing human relations at the highest level, and the power of spirituality to uplift humanity from its lower nature to that of spiritual triumph.

The Naqshbandi Sufi Tradition

Guidebook of Daily Practices and Devotions

By Shaykh Muhammad Hisham Kabbani

ISBN 1-930409-22-2, Paperback. 352 pp.

This book details the spiritual practices which have enabled devout seekers to awaken certainty of belief and to attain stations of nearness to the Divine Presence. The Naqshbandi Devotions are a source of light and energy, an oasis in a worldly desert. Through the manifestations of Divine Blessings bestowed on the practitioners of these magnificent rites, they will be granted the power of magnanimous healing, by which they seek to cure the hearts of mankind darkened by the gloom of spiritual poverty and materialism.

This detailed compilation, in English, Arabic and transliteration, includes the daily personal dhikr as well as the rites performed with every obligatory prayer, rites for holy days and details of the pilgrimage to Makkah and the visit of Prophet Muhammad in Madinah.

Naqshbandi Awrad
of Mawlana Shaykh Muhammad Nazim Adil al-Haqqani
Compiled by Shaykh Muhammad Hisham Kabbani
ISBN 1-930409-06-0, Paperback. 104 pp.

This book presents in detail, in both English, Arabic and transliteration, the daily, weekly and date-specific devotional rites of Naqshbandi practitioners, as prescribed by the world guide of the Naqshbandi-Haqqani Sufi Order, Mawlana Shaykh Muhammad Nazim Adil al-Haqqani.

Pearls and Coral, I & II
By Shaykh Muhammad Hisham Kabbani
ISBN 1-930409-07-9, Paperback. 220 pp.
ISBN 1-930409-08-7, Paperback. 220 pp.

A series of lectures on the unique teachings of the Naqshbandi Order, originating in the Near East and Central Asia, which has been highly influential in determining the course of human history in these regions. Always pushing aspirants on the path of Gnosis to seek higher stations of nearness to the God, the Naqshbandi Masters of Wisdom melded practical methods with deep spiritual wisdom to build an unequalled methodology of ascension to the Divine Presence.

The Sufi Science of Self-Realization

*A Guide to the Seventeen Ruinous Traits, the Ten Steps
to Discipleship and the Six Realities of the Heart*
By Shaykh Muhammad Hisham Kabbani
ISBN 1-930409-29-X, Paperback. 244 pp.

The path from submersion in the negative traits to the unveiling
of these six powers is known as migration to Perfected Character. Through a ten-step program, the author--a master of the
Naqshbandi Sufi Path--describes the science of eliminating the
seventeen ruinous characteristics of the tyrannical ego, to
achieve purification of the soul. The sincere seeker who follows
these steps, with devotion and discipline, will acheive an unveiling of the six powers which lie dormant within every human
heart.

Encyclopedia of Islamic Doctrine

Shaykh Muhammad Hisham Kabbani
ISBN: 1-871031-86-9, Paperback, Vol. 1-7.

The most comprehensive treatise on Islamic belief in the English
language. The only work of its kind in English, Shaykh Hisham
Kabbani's seven volume Encyclopedia of Islamic Doctrine is a
monumental work covering in great detail the subtle points of
Islamic belief and practice. Based on the four canonical schools
of thought, this is an excellent and vital resource to anyone seriously interested in spirituality. There is no doubt that in retro-
spect, this will be the most significant work of this age.

The Approach of Armageddon?

An Islamic Perspective
by Shaykh Muhammad Hisham Kabbani
ISBN 1-930409-20-6, Paperback 292 pp.

This unprecedented work is a "must read" for religious scholars and laypersons interested in broadening their understand-

ing of centuries-old religious traditions pertaining to the Last Days. This book chronicles scientific breakthroughs and world events of the Last Days as foretold by Prophet Muhammad. Also included are often concealed ancient predictions of Islam regarding the appearance of the anti-Christ, Armageddon, the leadership of believers by Mahdi ("the Savior"), the second coming of Jesus Christ, and the tribulations preceding the Day of Judgment. We are given final hope of a time on earth filled with peace, reconciliation, and prosperity; an age in which enmity and wars will end, while wealth is overflowing. No person shall be in need and the entire focus of life will be spirituality."

Keys to the Divine Kingdom
By Shaykh Muhammad Hisham Kabbani
ISBN 1-930409-28-1, Paperback. 140 pp.

God said, "We have created everything in pairs." This has to do with reality versus imitation. Our physical form here in this earthly life is only a reflection of our heavenly form. Like plastic fruit and real fruit, one is real, while the other is an imitation. This book looks at the nature of the physical world, the laws governing the universe and from this starting point, jumps into the realm of spiritual knowledge - Sufi teachings which must be "tasted" as opposed to read or spoken. It will serve to open up to the reader the mystical path of saints which takes human beings from the world of forms and senses to the world within the heart, the world of gnosis and spirituality - a world filled with wonders and blessings.

My Little Lore of Light
By Hajjah Amina Adil
ISBN 1-930409-35-4, Paperback, 204 pp.

A children's version of Hajjah Amina Adil's four volume work, *Lore Of Light*, this books relates the stories of God's prophets, from Adam to Muhammad, upon whom be peace, drawn from traditional Ottoman sources. This book is intended to be read aloud to young children and to be read by older children for themselves. The stories are shortened and simplified but not changed. The intention is to introduce young children to their prophets and to encourage thought and discussion in the family about the eternal wisdom these stories embody.

Muhammad: The Messenger of Islam
His Life and Prophecy
By Hajjah Amina Adil
ISBN 1-930409-11-7, Paperback. 608 pp.

Since the 7th century, the sacred biography of Islam's Prophet Muhammad has shaped the perception of the religion and its place in world history. This book skilfully etches the personal portrait of a man of incomparable moral and spiritual stature, as seen through the eyes of Muslims around the world. Compiled from classical Ottoman Turkish sources and translated into English, this comprehensive biography is deeply rooted in the life example of its prophet.

Printed in March 2024
by Rotomail Italia S.p.A., Vignate (MI) - Italy